Write 4 Today

Grade 4

Frank Schaffer Publications®

Editor: Linda Triemstra
Interior Designer: Lori Kibbey

Frank Schaffer Publications®

Send all inquiries to:
Frank Schaffer Publications
3195 Wilson Drive NW
Grand Rapids, Michigan 49534

Write 4 Today—grade 4

ISBN: 0-7682-3224-4

5 6 7 8 9 10 PAT 10 09 08 07

Write 4 Today

Table of Contents

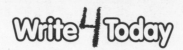

Introduction

Write 4 Today is a comprehensive yet quick and easy-to-use supplement sequenced to complement any fourth-grade writing curriculum. Essential writing skills and concepts are reviewed each day during a four-day period, with an evaluation each fifth day. This book supplies four concepts for four days covering a forty-week period. The focus alternates weekly between the mechanics of writing (capitalization, grammar, punctuation, and spelling) and the process of writing (prewriting/brainstorming, drafting, revising, and proofreading). A separate assessment is provided for the fifth day of each week.

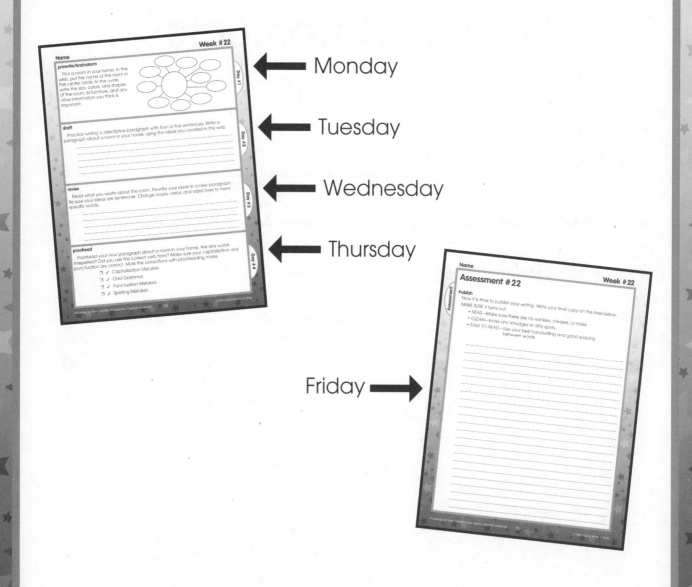

Monday

Tuesday

Wednesday

Thursday

Friday

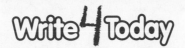

Because writing typically involves lengthier work than these short exercises require, many of the process exercises are ideal to use as springboards for more in-depth work. For example, if one task is creating an opening paragraph on a specific topic, the exercise could be expanded to include writing supporting paragraphs and a conclusion. A list of writing strategies, graphic organizers, and an editing checklist help students to hone their skills.

Answer keys are provided for daily drills and assessments (see pages 93–112). Concepts and skills are tested on an even/odd week rotation and follow a consistent format for ease of evaluation. Although the concepts and skills are individually categorized, most are interrelated so that many opportunities for practice and evaluation exist.

The daily approach of *Write 4 Today* provides risk-taking challenges, higher-level thinking exercises, problem-solving strategies, and necessary practice, emphasizing areas that frequently give students difficulty, such as punctuation and spelling. The program targets test-taking skills by incorporating the style and syntax of standardized tests.

For the even weeks, when the focus is on the writing process, use this ten-point rubric to assess the published work. You may cut and copy it onto the bottom of each assessment or attach it as a separate page. The rubric has been structured with a total of 10 possible points for each of the writing trait categories. These trait categories correlate with the popular 6 + 1 TRAITS* Writing Program (*a trademark of Northwest Regional Educational Laboratory) in this order from top to bottom: ideas, organization, voice, word choice, sentence fluency, conventions (covering all four COPS lines), and presentation. Use the rubric for student self assessments, peer assessments, or teacher assessments. Score the writing according to how often it clearly demonstrates each trait.

Never	Sometimes	Mostly	Always		**Grading Rubric**
1	4	7	10	**Focus**	Writing sticks to the topic with focused main ideas and supporting details
1	4	7	10	**Order**	Sentences and paragraphs have a clear order that makes sense to readers
1	4	7	10	**Tone**	Words and sentences use an interesting tone of voice that fits the audience and the writing style
1	4	7	10	**Vocabulary**	Writing uses a wide variety of vocabulary that is specific, accurate, strong, and original
1	4	7	10	**Flow**	Sentences are easy to read and flow smoothly from one to the next
1	4	7	10	**Details**	Capitalization is correct
1	4	7	10		Odd Grammar is corrected before publishing
1	4	7	10		Punctuation is correct
1	4	7	10		Spelling is correct
1	4	7	10	**Neatness**	Writing is neat, clean, and easy to read

Writing Strategies

Choose a **topic** for your writing.
- What am I writing about?

Decide on a **purpose** for writing.
- Why am I writing this piece?
- What do I hope the audience will learn from reading this piece?

Identify your **audience**.
- Who am I writing to?

Decide on a writing **style**.
- Expository—gives information or explains facts or ideas
- Persuasive—tries to talk someone into something
- Narrative—tells a story
- Descriptive—presents a clear picture of a person, place, thing, or idea

Decide on a **genre**—essay, letter, poetry, autobiography, fiction, nonfiction.

Decide on a **point of view**—first person, second person, or third person.

Brainstorm by listing or drawing your main ideas.

Use a graphic organizer to organize your thoughts.

Revise, revise, revise!
- Use **descriptive words**.
- Use **transitions** and linking expressions.
- Use a **variety of sentence structures**.
- **Elaborate** with facts and details.
- Group your ideas into **paragraphs**.
- **Proofread** for capitalization, punctuation, and spelling.

0-7682-3224-4 *Write 4 Today*

Clustering Planner

Clustering is a kind of graphic planner used to brainstorm ideas, images, and feelings around a specific word or concept.

How It Works: When clustering, you begin with a word, concept, topic, or question and work outward, linking and recording thoughts using text or pictures. As thoughts tumble out, you expand your ideas from the center like branches on a tree. When one branch stops or if an idea doesn't fit, create a new branch. Brainstorming clusters are free-flowing and can take any shape.

Word Web

A *word web* is a graphic planner that analyzes and gives alternatives for a specific word. Word webs are often used to list synonyms, antonyms, or rhyming words.

How it Works: A specific word is listed in the center. Alternatives for the word are written in the outer circles. There can be as many branches on a word web as needed.

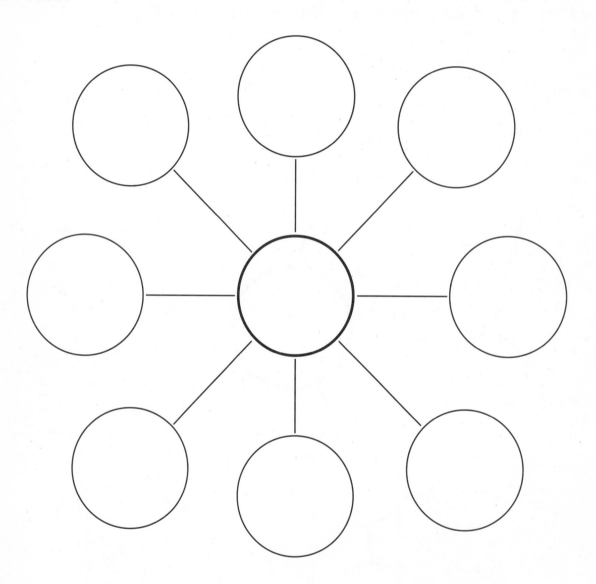

 0-7682-3224-4 *Write 4 Today*

Story Map

A *story map*, sometimes called a detail chart, is a graphic planner that lists vital information to be included in a news article, report, or informative story.

How it Works: Before writing begins, all of the important details are gathered and listed in an organized fashion. Mapping is a good way of making sure important facts are included in a story. The title or headline is the first line.

by:

Opening sentence:

Who?
What?
When?
Where?
Why or how?

Conclusion:

Venn Diagram

A *Venn diagram* is a graphic planner used for comparing and contrasting two things (people, places, events, ideas, and so on).

How It Works: Similarities and differences between things are organized by placing individual characteristics in either the left or right section and common characteristics within the overlapping section.

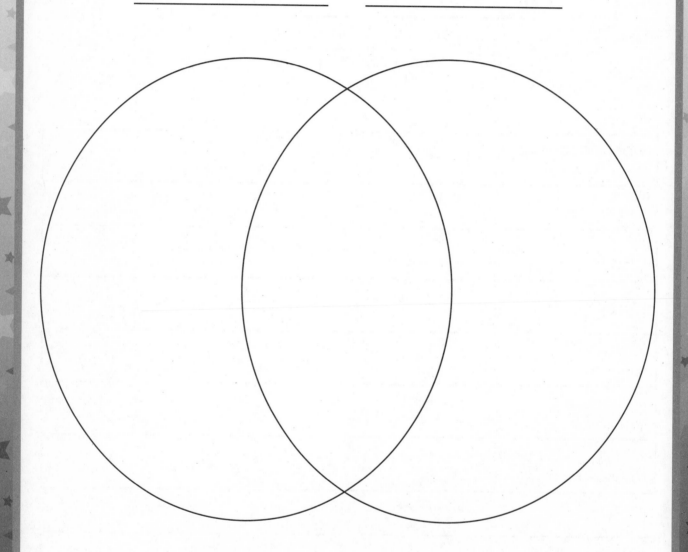

0-7682-3224-4 *Write 4 Today*

Paragraph Plan and Attribute Checklist

Paragraph Plan

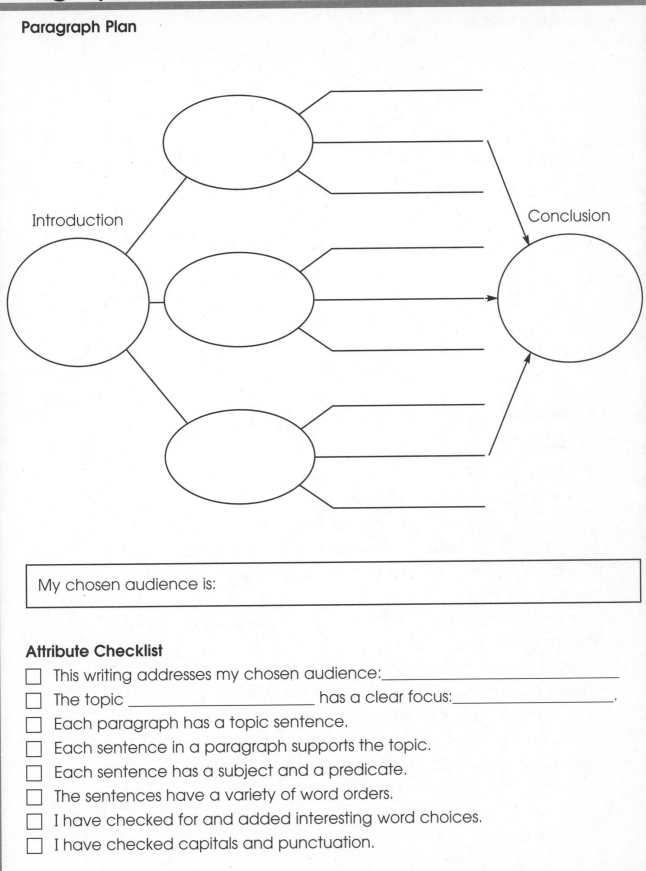

Introduction

Conclusion

My chosen audience is:

Attribute Checklist
- ☐ This writing addresses my chosen audience:_____
- ☐ The topic _____ has a clear focus:_____.
- ☐ Each paragraph has a topic sentence.
- ☐ Each sentence in a paragraph supports the topic.
- ☐ Each sentence has a subject and a predicate.
- ☐ The sentences have a variety of word orders.
- ☐ I have checked for and added interesting word choices.
- ☐ I have checked capitals and punctuation.

0-7682-3224-4 *Write 4 Today*

Editing Checklist

Proofreading Marks

Mark	Meaning	Mark	Meaning
Jen ∧	Insert word	JƎn	Lowercase
∧	Add a comma	jen ≡	Capitalize
⌄Jen⌄	Add quotation marks	¶	New paragraph
Jen⌄s	Add apostrophe	(stet)	Let it stand
Jen	Delete	(sp)	Spelling
⊙∧	Add period		

Make sure you

Capitalize the title.
Punctuate the title.
- Titles of long works are <u>underlined</u>.
- Titles of short works are in quotation marks. (" ")

Capitalize the first word in each sentence.
Capitalize proper nouns. (Sue, Texas, Monday)
Indent paragraphs.
Use quotation marks and commas with direct quotes. (He said, " ")
Use complete sentences.
Use the proper punctuation mark at the ends of sentences. (. ? !)
Use apostrophes in contractions. (I'm, don't, she'll)
Use apostrophes in possessive nouns. (Tim's bike)
Use commas in a series. (cats, dogs, and mice)
Use transitional words. (then, afterwards, meanwhile)
Use descriptive words. (bumpy, tiny, quick)

Published by Frank Schaffer Publications. Copyright protected.   0-7682-3224-4 *Write 4 Today*

Underline with three short lines the first letter of each word that should be capitalized in the sentence.

1. Did you watch the rose parade on new year's eve?

Fill in the blank with the correct form of the verb *be* (is, am, are).

2. I _____ going to the movies on Saturday.

Add the correct punctuation mark to the end of the sentence.

3. Do you want to go to the movies on Saturday night _____

Write the plural form for the following nouns.

4. tooth _____ woman _____ mouse _____

Underline with three short lines the first letter of each word that should be capitalized in the sentence.

1. The librarian helps us choose books during national book week.

Fill in the blank with the correct form of the verb *be* (is, am, are).

2. My friends _____ going with me.

Add the correct punctuation mark to the end of the sentence.

3. We are going to the theater at the mall _____

Write the plural form for the following nouns.

4. goose _____ person _____ deer _____

Underline with three short lines the first letter of each word that should be capitalized in the sentence.

1. My family eats turkey and potatoes on thanksgiving day.

Fill in the blank with the correct form of the verb *be* (is, am, are).

2. What _____ your phone number?

Add the correct punctuation mark to the end of the sentence.

3. I am going to buy a large popcorn and a bag of candy _____

Write the plural form for the following nouns.

4. child _____ sheep _____ man _____

Underline with three short lines the first letter of each word that should be capitalized in the sentence.

1. The class planted a tree on arbor day.

Fill in the blank with the correct form of the verb *be* (is, am, are).

2. You _____ a nice person.

Add the correct punctuation mark to the end of the sentence.

3. What do you like to eat at the movies _____

Write the plural form for the following nouns.

4. ox _____ moose _____ fish _____

Day #1

Day #2

Day #3

Day #4

Assessment #1

Underline with three short lines the first letter of each word that should begin with a capital letter. Put punctuation marks in the right places.

1. Our christmas tree is decorated with lights and ornaments

2. Did you watch the fireworks at the park on independence day

3. The irish celebrate st. patrick's day every year

4. What is your favorite halloween candy

Change these singular nouns into plural nouns.

5. calf _____

6. foot _____

7. child _____

Use each verb phrase in a short sentence.

8. am taking _____

_____

9. are going _____

_____

10. is reading _____

_____

prewrite/brainstorm

Meg started to make a list about what came to her mind when she thought about pickles. Part of her list is shown. What comes to your mind when you think about pickles? What would you add to Meg's list?

crunchy   sour   green   salty

_____   _____   _____   _____

_____   _____   _____   _____

draft

When you look at your list about pickles, you will want to focus on one main idea. Your first sentence might be

I like pickles because . . . _____

_____

Now write two or three more sentences about pickles. _____

_____

_____

revise

Look at your paragraph about pickles. Do all of the sentences talk about the same idea? What information could you add? What sentences would you change? Write out your changes.

_____

_____

_____

_____

_____

proofread

Look at your final paragraph about pickles. Are all of the words spelled correctly? Did you capitalize words that need to be capitalized? Proofread your paragraph.

- ❏ ✓ Capitalization Mistakes
- ❏ ✓ Odd Grammar
- ❏ ✓ Punctuation Mistakes
- ❏ ✓ Spelling Mistakes

Assessment # 2

Publish

Now it is time to publish your writing. Write your final copy on the lines below.
MAKE SURE it turns out:

- NEAT—Make sure there are no wrinkles, creases, or holes.
- CLEAN—Erase any smudges or dirty spots.
- EASY TO READ—Use your best handwriting and good spacing between words.

Use proofreading marks to fix the capitalization in this sentence.
1. Long before Europeans came to america, many different tribes settled the land.

Write the correct word (their, there, they're) in the blank.
2. _____ were many different tribes.

Add the missing commas.
3. We live in St. Ignace Michigan near the Museum of Ojibwa Culture.

Make the verbs past tense. **Example**: walk = walked
4. gather _____ look _____ paint _____

Use proofreading marks to fix the capitalization in this sentence.
1. The Iroquois lived in the mountains of new york and pennsylvania.

Write the correct word (their, there, they're) in the blank.
2. _____ homes were in the mountains.

Add the missing commas.
3. Famous tribes include the Iroquois the Ojibwa the Lakota and the Nez Percé tribes.

Make the verbs past tense. **Example**: tip = tipped
4. stop _____ wag _____ hum _____

Use proofreading marks to fix the capitalization in this sentence.
1. The Lakota tribe lived on the prairie in north Dakota and south dakota.

Write the correct word (their, there, they're) in the blank.
2. _____ studying the tribes of North America.

Add the missing commas.
3. In Idaho the Nez Percé was a peaceful tribe of traders and horse trainers.

Make the verbs past tense. **Example**: bake = baked
4. like _____ smile _____ share _____

Use proofreading marks to fix the capitalization in this sentence.
1. The city of Cheyenne was named for the Tribe that lived in Wyoming.

Write the correct word (their, there, they're) in the blank.
2. _____ were many Cheyenne tribes in Wyoming.

Add the missing commas.
3. A Native American burial mound is near the town of Aberdeen Ohio.

Make the verbs past tense. **Example**: cry = cried
4. try _____ hurry _____ study _____

Assessment #3

Correct the ten errors in the following paragraph.

Alyson rider liked to read about Native American People. She discovered that the

Ojibwa the Lakota and the Nez Percé all lived in tribes in America. She read about

Chief Joseph a famous nineteenth-century leader. She learn that red Cloud help

win land for the Lakota tribe. Alyson liked to read about the Cherokee and there

culture. She learned that their were Iroquois tribes that lived in the forest.

Now rewrite the paragraph correctly on the lines below.

_____

_____

_____

_____

_____

_____

_____

_____

_____

_____

_____

_____

_____

prewrite/brainstorm

Pick an activity that you are good at; it could be a sport, hobby, or skill. Put the name of the activity and the focus (good at) in the large oval. On the three lines, write what it is you are good at, why you believe you are good at it, and give a specific time you were good at this activity.

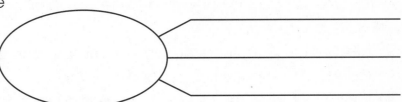

draft

Practice writing an introduction paragraph. Write a paragraph about what you are good at, using the three ideas you created in the list.

_____

_____

_____

_____

_____

revise

Read what you wrote yesterday. Rewrite your ideas in a new paragraph. Be sure your ideas are sentences. Change nouns, verbs, and adjectives to more specific words.

_____

_____

_____

_____

_____

proofread

Proofread your new paragraph. Are any words misspelled? Did you use the correct verb form? Make sure your capitalization and punctuation are correct. Mark the corrections with proofreading marks.

- ❏ ✓ Capitalization Mistakes
- ❏ ✓ Odd Grammar
- ❏ ✓ Punctuation Mistakes
- ❏ ✓ Spelling Mistakes

Assessment #4

Publish

Now it is time to publish your writing. Write your final copy on the lines below.

MAKE SURE it turns out:

- NEAT—Make sure there are no wrinkles, creases, or holes.
- CLEAN—Erase any smudges or dirty spots.
- EASY TO READ—Use your best handwriting and good spacing
  between words.

Read the beginning of the letter and use proofreading marks to fix the capitalization errors.

1. dear charlotte,
   thank you for your letter. it's fun to get mail!

Read the sentence and write the correct word (to, too, two) in the blank.

2. My dad needed _____ start his new job in Maine.

Write quotation marks around the exact words being said in the sentence.

3. José said, Birds don't have teeth.

Circle the correct word.

4. The past tense of **eat**:   ate   eight

Day #1

Read the sentence and use proofreading marks to fix the capitalization errors.

1. next week we are having "famous athlete day" in my class.

Read the sentence and write the correct word (to, too, two) in the blank.

2. We are driving to Maine in _____ weeks.

Write quotation marks around the exact words being said in the sentence.

3. What book are you reading? asked Michelle.

Circle the correct word.

4. The color of the sky: blew   blue

Day #2

Read the sentence and use proofreading marks to fix the capitalization errors.

1. my friend ebony is going to dress up as wilma rudolph, a famous runner and my teacher, ms. krull, is going to dress up as babe didrikson zaharias.

Read the sentence and write the correct word (to, too, two) in the blank.

2. My mom said six days is _____ long to spend in the car with the cats!

Write quotation marks around the exact words being said in the sentence.

3. Tina remarked, A flying fox is a type of bat.

Circle the correct word.

4. The opposite of **old**:   new   knew

Day #3

Read the sentence and use proofreading marks to fix the capitalization errors.

1. susan butcher won the iditarod sled dog race in alaska more than once.

Read the sentence and write the correct word (to, too, two) in the blank.

2. We all want _____ visit Niagra Falls.

Write quotation marks around the exact words being said in the sentence.

3. Wow! exclaimed Brandon. This book says a tiger shark may use up 12,000 teeth in five years.

Circle the correct word.

4. The number before two: won   one

Day #4

Assessment #5

Read the beginning of the letter and use proofreading marks to fix the capitalization errors.

1. dear hannah,

   we have to write someone a letter for school, so i picked you! what is new in kansas? write me back.

   your favorite cousin,
   charlotte

Write the correct word (to, too, two) in the blanks.

2. My dad left Colorado _____ months ago _____ start his new job.

3. My sister and I stayed here _____ finish the school year.

4. My mom is here, _____, of course.

Write quotation marks around the exact words being said.

5. What book are you reading? asked Tina.
6. *What Big Teeth You Have!* answered Brandon.
7. Michelle scowled. I don't have big teeth!
8. No, laughed Brandon. That's the title of the book.

Write the correct word for each blank.

9. At _____ (eight/ate) o'clock last night, the wind _____ (blue/blew) my mom's flower pot off the deck.

10. Madeleine _____ (knew/new) that her grandparents were visiting and couldn't wait to tell them that her team _____ (won/one) the soccer game.

prewrite/brainstorm

Put the name of the activity and why you believe you are good at it in the large oval. On the three lines, write three reasons you believe you are good at the activity.

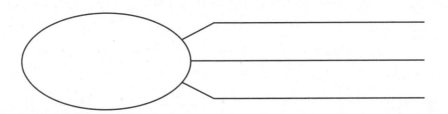

draft

Practice writing another supporting paragraph about the activity you are good at. Write a paragraph about why you are good at this activity, using the three ideas you created in the list.

_____

_____

_____

_____

_____

revise

Read what you wrote yesterday. Rewrite your ideas in a new paragraph. Be sure your ideas are sentences. Change nouns, verbs, and adjectives to more specific words.

_____

_____

_____

_____

_____

proofread

Proofread your new paragraph. Are any words misspelled? Did you use the correct verb form? Make sure your capitalization and punctuation are correct. Mark the corrections with proofreading marks.

- ☐ ✓ Capitalization Mistakes
- ☐ ✓ Odd Grammar
- ☐ ✓ Punctuation Mistakes
- ☐ ✓ Spelling Mistakes

Assessment #6

Publish

Now it is time to publish your writing. Write your final copy on the lines below.

MAKE SURE it turns out:

- NEAT—Make sure there are no wrinkles, creases, or holes.
- CLEAN—Erase any smudges or dirty spots.
- EASY TO READ—Use your best handwriting and good spacing between words.

_____

_____

_____

_____

_____

_____

_____

_____

_____

_____

_____

_____

_____

_____

_____

_____

_____

_____

_____

_____

Read the sentence and use proofreading marks to fix the capitalization errors.

1. Last summer my family took a trip to yellowstone national Park.

Write the correct abbreviation for the following words.

2. Doctor _____ December _____ Monday _____

Write the missing commas in the sentence.

3. Paul Bunyan was the biggest strongest and friendliest lumberjack ever.

Write the correct word (there, their, they're) in the blank.

4. The third graders are studying _____ community.

Read the sentence and use proofreading marks to fix the capitalization errors.

1. The huge park is in three states—wyoming, montana, and idaho.

Write the correct abbreviation for the following words.

2. Mister _____ January _____ Junior _____

Write the missing commas in the sentence.

3. Babe the blue ox was shaking shivering and shuddering when Paul Bunyan found him in a blue snowstorm.

Write the correct word (there, their, they're) in the blank.

4. _____ learning about ways children can get involved.

Read the sentence and use proofreading marks to fix the capitalization errors.

1. We camped at grand village beside yellowstone lake.

Write the correct abbreviation for the following words.

2. Senior _____ Street _____ Avenue _____

Write the missing commas in the sentence.

3. Johnny Appleseed wore a tin pot on his head a sack for a shirt and no shoes on his feet.

Write the correct word (there, their, they're) in the blank.

4. _____ is a homeless shelter near the school.

Read the sentence and use proofreading marks to fix the capitalization errors.

1. My brother, michael, and i had our own tent.

Write the correct abbreviation for the following words.

2. Boulevard _____ Road _____ February _____

Write the missing commas in the sentence.

3. John Henry was a strong brawny and muscular baby who was born with a hammer in his hand.

Write the correct word (there, their, they're) in the blank.

4. The third graders have decided to plant a garden for _____ service project.

Day #1

Day #2

Day #3

Day #4

Assessment #7

Read the sentences and use proofreading marks to fix the capitalization errors.

1. On the first day we were at yellowstone national Park, we went to see old Faithful.

2. Old faithful is a geyser that shoots up water about once an hour.

3. President teddy roosevelt used to ride horses at the park.

Write the names or phrases using the correct abbreviations.

4. Pennsylvania Avenue _____

5. Martin Luther King, Junior _____

6. Doctor McCandless _____

Write a sentence using commas to separate three items.

7. _____

Write three sentences using **there**, **their**, and **they're**.

8. _____

_____

9. _____

_____

10. _____

_____

prewrite/brainstorm

Put the name of the activity you are good at in the large oval. Write your three main ideas from your supporting paragraphs on the three lines.

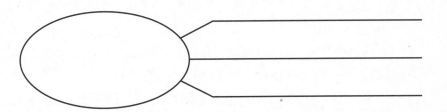

draft

Practice writing a concluding paragraph that sums up, or summarizes, the information you wrote about the activity you are good at. Use the three ideas you created in the list.

_____

_____

_____

_____

_____

revise

Read what you wrote yesterday. Rewrite your ideas in a new paragraph. Be sure your ideas are sentences. Change nouns, verbs, and adjectives to more specific words.

_____

_____

_____

_____

proofread

Proofread your new paragraph. Are any words misspelled? Did you use the correct verb form? Make sure your capitalization and punctuation are correct. Mark the corrections with proofreading marks.

- ❑ ✓ Capitalization Mistakes
- ❑ ✓ Odd Grammar
- ❑ ✓ Punctuation Mistakes
- ❑ ✓ Spelling Mistakes

Put all of the paragraphs together and see your five-paragraph writing!

Assessment #8

Publish

Now it is time to publish your writing. Write your final copy on the lines below.

MAKE SURE it turns out:

- NEAT—Make sure there are no wrinkles, creases, or holes.
- CLEAN—Erase any smudges or dirty spots.
- EASY TO READ—Use your best handwriting and good spacing between words.

_____

_____

_____

_____

_____

_____

_____

_____

_____

_____

_____

_____

_____

_____

_____

_____

_____

_____

_____

_____

Read the sentences and use proofreading marks to fix the capitalization errors.

1. who invented the airplane? i know many people were interested in airplanes.

Find and underline the groups of words that are not complete sentences.

2. Penguins are my favorite birds. I like the way they waddle. So cute!

Put commas, apostrophes, quotation marks, and underlining where they are needed.

3. Charlene read the book Sea Turtles last month.

Circle the correct word.

4. My (grate, great)-grandfather was a mayor.

Day # 1

Read the sentences and use proofreading marks to fix the capitalization errors.

1. on december 17, 1903, orville and wilbur wright flew their airplane.

Find and underline the groups of words that are not complete sentences.

2. Penguins cannot fly. They have flippers instead of wings. Are very good swimmers and divers.

Put commas, apostrophes, quotation marks, and underlining where they are needed.

3. When Charlene finished the book, she wrote a story called Turtles, Turtles, Turtles, and More Turtles!

Circle the correct word.

4. The (cent, scent, sent) of roasted turkey filled the kitchen.

Day # 2

Read the sentences and use proofreading marks to fix the capitalization errors.

1. the wright brothers must have had a wonderful christmas.

Find and underline the groups of words that are not complete sentences.

2. Many different kinds of penguins. Emperor penguins are the largest. Fairy penguins are the smallest.

Put commas, apostrophes, quotation marks, and underlining where they are needed.

3. What types of turtles did you read about? asked Valerie.

Circle the correct word.

4. It was so nice to (meet, meat, mete) the musician.

Day # 3

Read the sentences and use proofreading marks to fix the capitalization errors.

1. orville and wilbur lived in dayton, ohio.

Find and underline the groups of words that are not complete sentences.

2. Fairy penguins are a little more than one foot tall. Only weigh about two pounds.

Put commas, apostrophes, quotation marks, and underlining where they are needed.

3. I read about the leatherback the loggerhead the hawksbill and the green turtle she replied.

Circle the correct words.

4. Jeremiah (red, read) the (whole, hole) book in an (hour, our)!

Day # 4

Assessment # 9

Read the sentences and use proofreading marks to fix the capitalization errors and punctuation errors.

1. "when was the first nonstop flight across the atlantic ocean" i asked

2. "the english aviators, alcock and brown, flew from newfoundland to ireland in

   about sixteen hours in the year 1919," answered great-grandma

Find and underline the groups of words that are not complete sentences.

3. Someday I hope to visit Antarctica. Then see my favorite birds.

Rewrite the above groups of words to create one sentence.

4. _____

   _____

Put commas, apostrophes, quotation marks, and underlining where they are needed.

5. A leatherback turtles weight can be between 800 and 1,200 pounds

   said Charlene.

6. I don't believe it! exclaimed Valerie.

7. Valerie its true replied Charlene.

Circle the correct word or words for each sentence.

8. The man (rowed, road, rode) the boat slowly across the lake.

9. (Your, You're) going (to, too, two) the concert, (write, right)?

10. The (principal, principle) is the head of our school.

Name

prewrite/brainstorm

What does your dream car look like? Use the web to help you to describe your dream car.

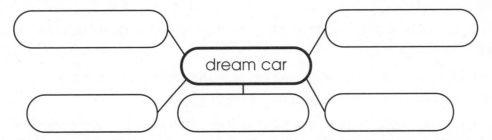

draft

Write a topic sentence about your dream car and then write three ideas based on your web.

_____

_____

_____

_____

_____

revise

Read what you wrote yesterday. Rewrite your ideas in a new paragraph. Be sure your ideas are sentences. Change nouns, verbs, and adjectives to more specific words.

_____

_____

_____

_____

_____

proofread

Proofread your new paragraph. Are any words misspelled? Did you use the correct verb form? Make sure your capitalization and punctuation are correct. Mark the corrections with proofreading marks.

- ❏ ✓ Capitalization Mistakes
- ❏ ✓ Odd Grammar
- ❏ ✓ Punctuation Mistakes
- ❏ ✓ Spelling Mistakes

Assessment

Assessment #10

Publish

Now it is time to publish your writing. Write your final copy on the lines below.
MAKE SURE it turns out:

- NEAT—Make sure there are no wrinkles, creases, or holes.
- CLEAN—Erase any smudges or dirty spots.
- EASY TO READ—Use your best handwriting and good spacing between words.

Underline with three short lines the first letter of each word that should be capitalized in the sentence.

1. The Gabriel family visited asia and europe last year.

Fill in the blank with the correct word.

2. May I borrow a piece _____ your paper? (of, off, from, off of)

This sentence needs a comma. Place the comma where it should be.

3. Many tourists visit beautiful London England.

Write the correct missing word in the blank.

4. Have you packed _____ new suitcase? (your/you're)

Underline with three short lines the first letter of each word that should be capitalized in the sentence.

1. Barbara found the chinese culture very interesting.

Fill in the blank with the correct word.

2. Please take your feet _____ the table. (of, off, off of)

This sentence needs commas. Place the commas where they should be.

3. Marianne said Beijing China was very busy.

Write the correct missing word in the blank.

4. I think _____ going to be tired. (your/you're)

Underline with three short lines the first letter of each word that should be capitalized in the sentence.

1. The Gabriels traveled to india and turkey.

Fill in the blank with the correct word.

2. "Don't jump _____ the train!" shouted Mrs. Gabriel. (of, off, off of)

This sentence needs a comma. Place the comma where it should be.

3. Mr. Gabriel said they arrived in Belgium on November 21 2004.

Write the correct missing word in the blank.

4. _____ not going to believe this story. (Your/You're)

Underline with three short lines the first letter of each word that should be capitalized in the sentence.

1. Marianne enjoyed the turkish food, but she didn't like the hot curry used in indian foods.

Fill in the blank with the correct word.

2. Barbara must _____ liked the hot food. (of, off, have)

This sentence needs commas. Place the commas where they should be.

3. The Gabriels were in Kyoto Japan from May 29 to June 2.

Write the correct missing word in the blank.

4. _____ vacation was an adventure. (Your/You're)

Day #1

Day #2

Day #3

Day #4

Assessment #11

Underline with three short lines the first letter of each word that should be capitalized in the sentence.

1. Marianne and Barbara made new friends on their trip through europe and asia.

2. They met a girl and boy from sweden.

3. When they traveled through spain, they all learned a little spanish.

Fill in the blanks with the correct words.

4. Fred borrowed some money _____ his friend. (of, off, from, off of)

5. That cup _____ cocoa tasted great! (of, off, from, off of)

6. I ought to _____ finished my homework. (of, off, have)

These sentences need commas. Place the commas where they should be.

7. Barbara really liked the people in Madrid Spain.

8. Several Central American countries declared their independence from Spain on September 15 1821.

Write the correct missing words (your/you're) in the blanks.

9. _____ sister said _____ going on another vacation next year.

prewrite/brainstorm

What is your favorite vacation spot? Write a list of all the things you can think about why you like that place.

_____

_____

_____

_____

_____

draft

When you look at your list about your favorite vacation spot, you will want to focus on one main idea. Your first sentence might be

My favorite place to go on vacation is (name the place) because . . . _____

_____

Now write two or three more sentences about yor favorite vacation spot.

_____

_____

revise

Look at your paragraph about your favorite vacation spot. Do all of the sentences talk about the same idea? What information could you add? What sentences would you change? Write out your changes.

_____

_____

_____

_____

_____

proofread

Look at your final paragraph about your favorite vacation spot. Are all of the words spelled correctly? Did you capitalize words that need to be capitalized? Proofread your paragraph.

- ☐ ✓ Capitalization Mistakes
- ☐ ✓ Odd Grammar
- ☐ ✓ Punctuation Mistakes
- ☐ ✓ Spelling Mistakes

Assessment #12

Publish

Now it is time to publish your writing. Write your final copy on the lines below.

MAKE SURE it turns out:

- NEAT—Make sure there are no wrinkles, creases, or holes.
- CLEAN—Erase any smudges or dirty spots.
- EASY TO READ—Use your best handwriting and good spacing between words.

Underline with three short lines the first letter of each word that should begin with a capital letter.

1. "i need to see miss nancy wynters in my office," said mrs. veirling.

Pick the correct word (it's/its) for the sentence.

2. Nancy wanted to see the blue fish in _____ aquarium.

Put quotation marks where they belong around the direct quote in the sentence.

3. What a hot day! exclaimed Jerome.

Fill in the circle next to the correct word for the sentence.

4. Please fill this ____ with water.   ○ picture   ○ pitcher

Underline with three short lines the first letter of each word that should begin with a capital letter.

1. i am going to finish my book report tonight.

Pick the correct word (It's/Its) for the sentence.

2 _____ a report on the book *Island of the Blue Dolphins*.

Put quotation marks where they belong around the direct quote in the sentence.

3. Sam, would you like to go swimming? he asked.

Fill in the circle next to the correct word for the sentence.

4. Coyotes live in the ____.   ○ desert   ○ dessert

Underline with three short lines the first letter of each word that should begin with a capital letter.

1. mr. brown would like you to complete your homework for next week.

Pick the correct word (it's/its) for the sentence.

2. The cat likes sleeping in _____ bed.

Put quotation marks where they belong around the direct quote in the sentence.

3. Let's ride our bikes to the pond, said Jerome.

Fill in the circle next to the correct word for the sentence.

4. He chopped the onions so ____ that I couldn't taste them.   ○ finally   ○ finely

---

Underline with three short lines the first letter of each word that should begin with a capital letter.

1. "we are flying to see my aunt, professor egan, in virginia," said francine.

Pick the correct word (it's/its) for the sentence.

2. She said _____ a four-hour flight.

Put quotation marks where they belong around the direct quote in the sentence.

3. I need, said Sam, to get my swim trunks and a towel.

Fill in the circle next to the correct word for the sentence.

4. I like every flavor ____ mint chip.   ○ accept   ○ except

Assessment #13

Underline with three short lines the first letter of each word that should begin with a capital letter.

1. mrs. orloff and mrs. wynters were waiting for the girls in the office. the

   principal, mrs. vierling, was also there.

2. they needed to talk to miss Francine jones.

Pick the correct word (it's/its) for the sentence.

3. "I hope _____ going to be good news," Francine said.

4. "We want to talk to you about the dog and _____ puppies," she said.

Put quotation marks where they belong around the direct quote in the sentence.

5. Do you want to take the short cut by Mill Park? asked Sam.

6. I've heard that the bridge through Mill Park is unsafe, said Jerome.

7. Well, replied Sam, let's not go that way.

The words look and sound similar but have different meanings. Pick the correct word.

8. My sister loves any kind of _____ (desert/dessert) as long as it is sweet.

9. We _____ (finely/finally) were ready to start our vacation.

10. Eddie agree to _____ (accept/except) my help with his homework.

Name

prewrite/brainstorm

Remember writing about your favorite vacation spot? Today you're going to write another supporting paragraph about why you like the spot.

Start by looking at your list of three reasons why you like that place. Pick one of the reasons you didn't write about yet and make a list of examples that support your idea.

_____

_____

_____

Day #1

draft

Look at your list about your favorite vacation spot. Taking the ideas you wrote, create three or four sentences about them.

_____

_____

_____

_____

Day #2

revise

Look at your supporting paragraph about your favorite vacation spot. Do all of the sentences talk about the same idea? What information could you add? What sentences would you change? Write out your changes.

_____

_____

_____

_____

Day #3

proofread

Look at your supporting paragraph about your favorite vacation spot. Are all of the words spelled correctly? Did you capitalize words that need to be capitalized? Proofread your paragraph.

    ❏ ✓ Capitalization Mistakes

    ❏ ✓ Odd Grammar

    ❏ ✓ Punctuation Mistakes

    ❏ ✓ Spelling Mistakes

Day #4

Assessment

Assessment #14

Publish

Now it is time to publish your writing. Write your final copy on the lines below.

MAKE SURE it turns out:

- NEAT—Make sure there are no wrinkles, creases, or holes.
- CLEAN—Erase any smudges or dirty spots.
- EASY TO READ—Use your best handwriting and good spacing between words.

A proper noun names a special person, place, or thing. Begin each proper noun with a capital letter.

1. california _____ holiday _____ first avenue _____

Change the sentence fragment into a sentence.

2. My wrist watch _____.

A comma is needed in this sentence. Put it in the correct place.

3. Along with helping you remember things a journal helps you learn to write better.

Write the correct word in the blank.

4. My family is planning a trip to _____ York State. (Knew/New)

Day #1

A proper noun names a special person, place, or thing. Begin each proper noun with a capital letter.

1. mr. johnson _____ thanksgiving _____ school _____

Change the sentence fragment into a sentence.

2. _____ likes to skate.

Add or delete commas in this sentence.

3. For example say you wanted to write about a funny experience, you had at school.

Write the correct word in the blank.

4. We each get to pick _____ place to visit. (one/won)

Day #2

A proper noun names a special person, place, or thing. Begin each proper noun with a capital letter.

1. laura _____ january _____ harvard college _____

Change the sentence fragment into a sentence.

2. Mr. Bamberger's dog _____.

A comma is needed in this sentence. Put it in the correct place.

3. My journal is about my life in Denver Colorado.

Write the correct word in the blank.

4. My mom _____ to see the Statue of Liberty. (wants/once)

Day #3

A proper noun names a special person, place, or thing. Begin each proper noun with a capital letter.

1. street _____ idaho _____ egypt _____

Change the sentence fragment into a sentence.

2. _____ two pencils and a ruler.

Add or delete commas in this sentence.

3. You can look up your story, in your journal, and you can read about it.

Write the correct word in the blank.

4. My dad plans _____ visit the Guggenheim Museum. (to/too/two)

Day #4

Assessment #15

A common noun names any person, place, or thing. A proper noun names a special person, place, or thing. Which nouns are proper nouns? Begin each proper noun with a capital letter.

1. russia _____

2. river _____

3. monday _____

Change the sentence fragment into a sentence.

4. _____ came in the front door.

5. Mother and Father _____ .

Add or delete commas in these sentences.

6. I have my second-grade journals and I have a journal from third grade.

7. My teacher gave me a new blank book and I used it to start a journal.

Write the correct words in the blanks.

8. And me, _____ do I want to visit? (where/wear)

9. I thought it over _____ a long time. (four/for)

10. I _____ like to see Niagra Falls. (wood/would)

prewrite/brainstorm

Now it's time to write a concluding paragraph about your favorite vacation spot. Go back over your introductory paragraph and your three supporting paragraphs and make a list of your main points. You should have three main points, one for each supporting paragraph.

_____

_____

_____

_____

draft

You want your concluding paragraph to sum up what you've written about why you like your favorite vacation spot. Write a paragraph using the three main points that summarizes your main points.

_____

_____

_____

_____

_____

revise

Look at your concluding paragraph about your favorite vacation spot. Do the sentences talk about why you like your vacation spot? What information could you add? What sentences would you change? Write out your changes.

_____

_____

_____

_____

_____

proofread

Look at your final paragraph about your favorite vacation spot. Are all of the words spelled correctly? Did you capitalize words that need to be capitalized? Proofread your paragraph.

- ❏ ✓ Capitalization Mistakes
- ❏ ✓ Odd Grammar
- ❏ ✓ Punctuation Mistakes
- ❏ ✓ Spelling Mistakes

Day #1

Day #2

Day #3

Day #4

Assessment #16

Publish

Now it is time to publish your writing. Write your final copy on the lines below.
MAKE SURE it turns out:

- NEAT—Make sure there are no wrinkles, creases, or holes.
- CLEAN—Erase any smudges or dirty spots.
- EASY TO READ—Use your best handwriting and good spacing between words.

Day #1

Underline with three short lines the first letter of each word that should be capitalized.

1. dear dr. doolittle,

Put the correct word in the blank.

2. Have you met _____ (your/you're) new neighbor's cat?

Use proofreading marks to correct the punctuation.

3. Carrie looked across the prairie from her doorstep! The prairie looked like the sea

Read the clue and write the homphone in the blank.

4. The vehicle word that is a homophone for **plain**: _____

Day #2

Underline with three short lines the first letter of each word that should be capitalized.

1. i have a terrible toothache. my friend charlie chipmunk told me you help animals.

Put the correct word in the blank.

2. _____ (Its/ It's) the strangest cat I have ever seen.

Use proofreading marks to correct the punctuation.

3. How I miss the shade thought Carrie and how I miss our old home!

Read the clue and write the homphone in the blank.

4. The time word that is a homophone for **weak**: _____

Day #3

Underline with three short lines the first letter of each word that should be capitalized.

1. Could i come see you this thursday?

Put the correct word in the blank.

2. I think it is chasing _____ (your/you're) dog Rufus.

Use proofreading marks to correct the punctuation.

3. It was early in the morning but already it was hot

Read the clue and write the homphone in the blank.

4. The homophone for **hare** is _____.

Day #4

Underline with three short lines the first letter of each word that should be capitalized.

1. yours truly,

    buddy beaver

Put the correct word in the blank.

2. Let's bark at the cat like Rufus would to get _____ (its/it's) attention.

Use proofreading marks to correct the punctuation.

3. Carrie! called Mama from the fireplace Please come and help me with breakfast

Read the clue and write the homphones in the blank.

4. Two homophones for **two**: _____

Assessment #17

Proofread the letter for capitalization, grammar, punctuation, and spelling errors.

april 1 2003

dear Aesop

why did you have to make up that foolish story The Tortoise and the Hare I am so tired of it.

The hairs in my family have always been speed champions. yet every time a child hears you're story, I lose the race to a poky tortoise. Its not fair!

Couldnt you have made the story "Aesop and the tortoise" or "The Cheetah and the Hare"?

Then maybe my dear mom wouldn't say to me, That Aesop is a terrible storyteller.

Instead i spend my life hopping from library to library, adding pages to books so that I win the race

I must go now. I need to write a letter to ms. beatrix Potter.

Thank you for your time.

yours truly

Hare

prewrite/brainstorm

What materials do you need to write a letter? Brainstorm about your topic by writing the supplies you use to write a letter.

MATERIALS

_____   _____   _____

_____   _____   _____

_____   _____   _____

draft

Practice writing a paragraph that explains what materials are needed to write a letter. Begin your paragraph with a topic sentence. Use the items you listed when you brainstormed.

_____

_____

_____

_____

_____

revise

Read what you wrote yesterday. Rewrite your ideas in a new paragraph. Be sure your ideas are sentences. Change nouns, verbs, and adjectives to more specific words.

_____

_____

_____

_____

_____

proofread

Proofread your new paragraph. Are any words misspelled? Did you use the correct verb form? Make sure your capitalization and punctuation are correct. Mark the corrections with proofreading marks.

- ❑ ✓ Capitalization Mistakes
- ❑ ✓ Odd Grammar
- ❑ ✓ Punctuation Mistakes
- ❑ ✓ Spelling Mistakes

Assessment

Assessment #18

Publish

Now it is time to publish your writing. Write your final copy on the lines below.

MAKE SURE it turns out:

- NEAT—Make sure there are no wrinkles, creases, or holes.
- CLEAN—Erase any smudges or dirty spots.
- EASY TO READ—Use your best handwriting and good spacing between words.

_____

_____

_____

_____

_____

_____

_____

_____

_____

_____

_____

_____

_____

_____

_____

_____

_____

_____

Use proofing marks to show letters that should be capitalized or lowercase.

1. Rosa parks was a brave African-american woman who helped make our Country a better place.

Circle the best phrase to replace the underlined phrase.

2. Everybody knows I <u>didn't mean nothing</u> by it.
   a. did mean nothing   b. didn't mean none   c. didn't mean anything

Circle the correct choice for the missing punctuation.

3. Ms. Rodriguez showed us a picture of Henry Hudson.   a. ?   b. ,   c. None

Circle the choice that shows the right spelling of the missing word.

4. This _____ is for gym.   a. uniforme   b. unifurm   c. uniform

Use proofing marks to show letters that should be capitalized or lowercase.

1. Until 1955, african-american people in montgomery, Alabama, had to give up their bus seats to white People.

Circle the best phrase to replace the underlined phrase.

2. You <u>haven't seen nothing</u> yet.
   a. have seen nothing   b. haven't seen none   c. haven't seen anything

Circle the correct choice for the missing punctuation.

3. What area did Henry Hudson explore   a. .   b. ?   c. None

Circle the choice that shows the right spelling of the missing word.

4. That dress costs three _____ dollars!   a. hundred   b. hunedred   c. hunderd

Use proofing marks to show letters that should be capitalized or lowercase.

1. Rosa parks believed that this city law was wrong, and one day She said she would not give up her Seat.

Circle the best phrase to replace the underlined phrase.

2. This <u>isn't any good neither</u>.
   a. isn't none good neither   b. isn't any good either   c. isn't nothing good neither

Circle the correct choice for the missing punctuation.

3. We re going to draw a map of explorers' routes.   a. .   b. '   c. None

Circle the choice that shows the right spelling of the missing word.

4. Did you finish the _____ yet?   a. blous   b. blousse   c. blouse

Use proofing marks to show letters that should be capitalized or lowercase.

1. Rosa parks was arrested for not giving up her Seat.

Circle the best phrase to replace the underlined phrase.

2. He <u>wouldn't do no work</u>.
   a. wouldn't do any work   b. would not do no work   c. would do any work

Circle the correct choice for the missing punctuation.

3. I want to see Baltimore Maryland, on the Chesapeake Bay.   a. ,   b. !   c. None

Circle the choice that shows the right spelling of the missing word.

4. My new shirt has _____ on it.   a. daisies   b. daisys   c. daises

Assessment #19

Use proofreading marks to show which letters should be capitalized or lowercase.

1. Many americans were very angry that Rosa was arrested. She had stood up—
   rather, she had sat down—for what was fair and Right.

2. Finally, the United states Supreme court said that the city's bus law
   was wrong.

3. Because of Rosa parks's bravery, a wrong was turned into a Right.

Circle the best phrase to replace the underlined phrase.

4. I <u>couldn't find it nowhere</u>.

   a. could find it nowhere
   b. couldn't find it nohow
   c. couldn't find it anywhere

Write a new sentence to correct the double negative in the sentence.

5. I didn't have no money. _____

Mark the sentences for missing punctuation.

6. Along with his son Hudson was set adrift in a boat

7. We ll never know what happened to them.

8. You can drive to Hudson Bay, through Ontario Canada.

Circle the choice that shows the right spelling of the missing word.

9. He _____ stained his jacket.

   a. acidentaly
   b. accidentally
   c. acdentaly

Use proofreading marks to fix the spelling in this sentence.

10. Everyone loves to waer blue jeens.

prewrite/brainstorm

How much television do you watch? What shows do you like? Do you watch television with your family? Do you think television is good for family life? Why or why not? Think about these questions and write down your ideas.

_____

_____

_____

_____

_____

draft

A narrative paragraph tells a story. Write a narrative paragraph about you and your television based on the list you wrote.

_____

_____

_____

_____

_____

revise

Read your paragraph about television. Does it tell a story? Does it show your ideas about television? Are your main points clear? Rewrite the paragraph using specific nouns, verbs, and adjectives to help make your paragraph clear.

_____

_____

_____

_____

_____

proofread

Read your paragraph about television one more time. Proofread it for spelling, punctuation, grammar, and capitalization.

- ☐ ✓ Capitalization Mistakes
- ☐ ✓ Odd Grammar
- ☐ ✓ Punctuation Mistakes
- ☐ ✓ Spelling Mistakes

Assessment #20

Assessment

Publish

Now it is time to publish your writing. Write your final copy on the lines below.

MAKE SURE it turns out:

- NEAT—Make sure there are no wrinkles, creases, or holes.
- CLEAN—Erase any smudges or dirty spots.
- EASY TO READ—Use your best handwriting and good spacing between words.

Underline with three short lines the first letter of each word that should be capitalized.

1. Morgan Freeman starred in a movie with Jim Carrey called *bruce almighty*.

Underline the predicate in the sentence.

2. Sunshine warms the soil. Then the rain falls.

Add commas where they are needed.

3. Large mammals such as bears bobcats and deer live in the Appalachian Mountains.

Put a line through the word that is not spelled correctly. Write the correct spelling in the blank.

4. George Washington Carver was an African-American scintist. _____

Day #1

Underline with three short lines the first letter of each word that should be capitalized.

1. Michael Jackson's album *thriller* sold over 45 million copies.

Underline the predicate in the sentence.

2. A seed absorbs water and swells. The swelling splits the seed coat open.

Add commas where they are needed.

3. Pines and junipers grow on the lower slopes of the Rocky Mountains but firs and spruce grow on the higher areas.

Put a line through the word that is not spelled correctly. Write the correct spelling in the blank.

4. As a boy Carver was always intrested in learning. _____

Day #2

Underline with three short lines the first letter of each word that should be capitalized.

1. Writer Alice Walker won a Pulitzer Prize for her novel *the color purple*.

Underline the predicate in the sentence.

2. Roots appear and anchor the seed in the soil. Next, a shoot appears.

Add commas where they are needed.

3. Farmers in the Appalachian Mountains grow corn grow tobacco and raise poultry.

Put a line through the word that is not spelled correctly. Write the correct spelling in the blank.

4. Carver graduated from colege in 1894 with a degree in agriculture. _____

Day #3

Underline with three short lines the first letter of each word that should be capitalized.

1. W. C. Handy wrote the song "st. louis blues" in 1914.

Underline the predicate in the sentence.

2. The shoot curves upward and pulls the seed leaves with it. Then the shoot straightens.

Add commas where they are needed.

3. Goats and bighorn sheep live in the mountains but coyotes and moose live in the valleys.

Put a line through the word that is not spelled correctly. Write the correct spelling in the blank.

4. After 1914, he began research on penuts, pecans, and sweet potatoes. _____

Day #4

Assessment # 21

Underline with three short lines the first letter of each word that should be capitalized.

1. Bill Cosby starred in a television program called *the cosby show* for many years.

2. Maya Angelou wrote a book called *i know why the caged bird sings.*

3. Eddie Murphy starred in *dr. doolittle* and *the nutty professor.*

Underline the predicate in the sentences.

4. The young plant needs water, sunshine, minerals, oxygen, and carbon dioxide to grow well.

5. Minerals come from the soil around the plant's roots.

6. They dissolve in water absorbed by the roots.

Add commas to the following sentences where they are needed.

7. The Appalachian Mountains have rich mineral deposits important agricultural regions and recreational areas.

8. The Rocky Mountains run through New Mexico Colorado Utah Wyoming Idaho Montana Washington and Alaska.

Put a line through the words that are not spelled correctly. Then rewrite the sentence with correct spelling.

9. Carver developed three hundred products from penuts, including face powder, soap, ink, and a milk substatute.

   _____

   _____

10. George Washington Carver recieved many awards and honors for his contributions to schience.

    _____

    _____

prewrite/brainstorm

Pick a room in your home. In the web, put the name of the room in the center circle. In the ovals, write the size, colors, and shapes of the room, its furniture, and any other information you think is important.

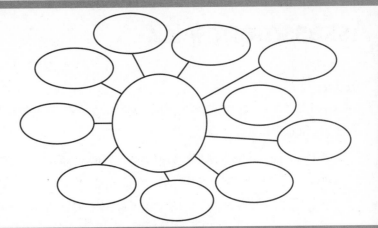

draft

Practice writing a descriptive paragraph with four or five sentences. Write a paragraph about a room in your house, using the ideas you created in the web.

_____
_____
_____
_____
_____

revise

Read what you wrote about the room. Rewrite your ideas in a new paragraph. Be sure your ideas are sentences. Change nouns, verbs, and adjectives to more specific words.

_____
_____
_____
_____
_____

proofread

Proofread your new paragraph about a room in your home. Are any words misspelled? Did you use the correct verb form? Make sure your capitalization and punctuation are correct. Mark the corrections with proofreading marks.

- ❒ ✓ Capitalization Mistakes
- ❒ ✓ Odd Grammar
- ❒ ✓ Punctuation Mistakes
- ❒ ✓ Spelling Mistakes

Assessment # 22

Publish

Now it is time to publish your writing. Write your final copy on the lines below.

MAKE SURE it turns out:

- NEAT—Make sure there are no wrinkles, creases, or holes.
- CLEAN—Erase any smudges or dirty spots.
- EASY TO READ—Use your best handwriting and good spacing between words.

_____

_____

_____

_____

_____

_____

_____

_____

_____

_____

_____

_____

_____

_____

_____

_____

_____

_____

Circle the choice that shows the right capitalization.

1. a. Janna's recital is Tuesday, october 24.
    b. Janna's recital is tuesday, october 24.
    c. Janna's recital is Tuesday, October 24.

Circle the word that works in both sentences.

2. The player began to _____ .
    Put the new _____ on the car.
    a. run
    b. fender
    c. weaken
    d. tire

Add the correct punctuation to the sentence.

3. What do you think students should write about _____

Make the verbs past tense.
    Example: walk = walked

4. kick _____

    play _____

    answer _____

Circle the choice that shows the right capitalization.

1. a. Janna has ballet on mondays.
    b. Janna has ballet on Mondays.
    c. Janna has Ballet on Mondays.

Circle the word that works in both sentences.

2. Do you feel _____ ?
    We get our water from a _____ .
    a. well
    b. good
    c. pipe
    d. sick

Add the correct punctuation to the sentence.

3. If you said, "Things that they know," you are right _____

Make the verbs past tense.
    Example: tip = tipped

4. rub _____

    clap _____

    drag _____

Circle the choice that shows the right capitalization.

1. a. Janna dances from september to May.
    b. Janna dances from September to May.
    c. Janna dances from september to may.

Circle the word that works in both sentences.

2. Mrs. Johnson said Carrie was a _____ student.
    The light from the headlights was _____ .
    a. noisy
    b. red
    c. bright
    d. hardworking

Add the correct punctuation to the sentence.

3. It is easy to write about things we know _____

Make the verbs past tense.
    Example: bake = baked

4. skate _____

    race _____

    dribble _____

Circle the choice that shows the right capitalization.

1. a. Janna is going to a concert on friday, April 4.
    b. Janna is going to a Concert on friday, April 4.
    c. Janna is going to a concert on Friday, April 4.

Circle the word that works in both sentences.

2. The surface of the car was _____ .
    Mr. Abed gave a _____ speech.
    a. red
    b. dirty
    c. painted
    d. dull

Add the correct punctuation to the sentence.

3. Do you think you can get ideas from your hobbies, family, friends, and school events _____

Make the verbs past tense.
    Example: cry = cried

4. multiply _____

    marry _____

    fry _____

Assessment # 23

Put punctuation marks at the end of the sentences. Use a period, a question mark, or an exclamation mark. Underline with three short lines the first letter of each word that should be capitalized.

1. shadow puppets perform behind a screen or sheet _____

2. light shines from above and behind the puppets to create shadows on the screen _____

3. did you know that light travels in a straight line _____

4. what is a shadow _____

5. a shadow is the area of shade on a flat surface made by an object that blocks light _____

Choose the answer in which the underlined word is used the same way in the sentence.

6. Please file these papers.

   a. The counselor pulled out her file on the Jones family.
   b. Sally used a file to smooth her fingernails.
   c. I put the file cards in order.
   d. Jane asked her secretary to file the reports on water safety.

7. She could not reach the right note on the piano.

   a. Please make a note of this change.
   b. I wrote a note so you will not forget.
   c. The musical note he asked us to play was C.
   d. Note the large size of the buildings.

Make the verbs past tense.

8. talk _____   brush _____

9. flip _____   rob _____

10. dry _____   carry _____

prewrite/brainstorm

In a persuasive paragraph, the writer tries to persuade the reader to do something or think a certain way. Begin to create a persuasive paragraph. Today, list the reasons you think your mother should let you get a dog.

_____

_____

_____

_____

_____

draft

Using your list of reasons you think your mother should let you get a dog, write a persuasive paragraph. Remember to use a topic sentence and a concluding sentence.

_____

_____

_____

_____

_____

revise

Look at the paragraph you wrote about getting a dog. Is it persuasive? Does it have a topic sentence? Does it have points that fit your topic sentence? Did you write a concluding sentence? Rewrite your paragraph, and make your words more specific.

_____

_____

_____

_____

proofread

Now it's time to proofread your persuasive paragraph. Look at your final paragraph. Are all of the words spelled correctly? Did you capitalize words that need to be capitalized? Did you use the correct verbs and nouns? Proofread your paragraph.

- ☐ ✓ Capitalization Mistakes
- ☐ ✓ Odd Grammar
- ☐ ✓ Punctuation Mistakes
- ☐ ✓ Spelling Mistakes

Assessment

Assessment #24

Publish

Now it is time to publish your writing. Write your final copy on the lines below.

MAKE SURE it turns out:

- NEAT—Make sure there are no wrinkles, creases, or holes.
- CLEAN—Erase any smudges or dirty spots.
- EASY TO READ—Use your best handwriting and good spacing between words.

Underline with three short lines the first letter of each word that should be capitalized.

1. the north American grizzly bear is rare in the United states.

Underline the correct form of the present-tense verb in the sentence.

2. Every day I (jog, jogs) in the park.

Add the correct punctuation to the quotation.

3. Benjamin Franklin said Early to bed and early to rise makes a man healthy wealthy and wise

Combine the word with the suffix to make an abstract noun.

4. citizen + -ship = _____   imagine + -ation = _____

Underline with three short lines the first letter of each word that should be capitalized.

1. panda bears from china are not really bears.

Underline the correct form of the present-tense verb in the sentence.

2. My brother (run, runs) three miles before school.

Add the correct punctuation to the quotation.

3. Nature wears one universal grin stated Henry Fielding

Combine the word with the suffix to make an abstract noun.

4. connect + -tion = _____   friendly + -ness = _____

Underline with three short lines the first letter of each word that should be capitalized.

1. the stuffed teddy bear was named after president theodore roosevelt.

Underline the correct form of the present-tense verb in the sentence.

2. He (go, goes) around the park four times.

Add the correct punctuation to the quotation.

3. I am always doing that which I can not do in order that I may learn to do it Pablo Picasso stated

Combine the word with the suffix to make an abstract noun.

4. free + -dom = _____   explore + -ation = _____

Underline with three short lines the first letter of each word that should be capitalized.

1. brown bears are found in asia, europe, and north america.

Underline the correct form of the present-tense verb in the sentence.

2. My two golden retrievers usually (scurry, scurries) next to me as I jog.

Add the correct punctuation to the quotation.

3. All sorrows can be borne if you put them into a story or tell a story about them Isak Dinesen, the Danish author wrote

Combine the word with the suffix to make an abstract noun.

4. happy + -ness = _____   inform + -ation = _____

Assessment # 25

Write two sentences about bears. Be sure to use correct capitalization.

1. _____

2. _____

Underline the correct form of the present-tense verb in the sentence.

3. Sometimes my dogs (take, takes) off after a squirrel.

4. Two police officers always (pass, passes) us in the park.

5. They (smile, smiles) and (wave, waves) at us.

Add the correct punctuation to the quotation.

6. All for one and one for all wrote Alexandre Dumas, the French dramatist. It was the Musketeers' motto in *The Three Musketeers*.

Combine the word with the suffix to make an abstract noun.

7. ill + -ness = _____

8. king + -dom = _____

9. punish + -ment = _____

10. pollute + -tion = _____

prewrite/brainstorm

Narrative writing tells a story. To plan a story, you use a story map. You need characters, a setting, and a problem. Next, you need events and a solution. Here are your characters, setting, and problem: You and your best friend are at the beach on Saturday, and you find a bottle with a treasure map inside. You don't know if it's real or not. Write a list of three events and a solution based on this information.

Event 1	Event 2	Event 3	Solution

draft

Write an introductory paragraph about you, your friend, and the treasure map you found on the beach.

_____

_____

_____

_____

_____

revise

Read your introductory paragraph. Does it have a topic sentence? Does it have points that fit your topic sentence? Rewrite your paragraph, and make your words more specific.

_____

_____

_____

_____

proofread

Now it's time to proofread your introductory paragraph. Are all of the words spelled correctly? Did you capitalize words that need to be capitalized? Did you use the correct verbs and nouns? Proofread your paragraph.

- ❏ ✓ Capitalization Mistakes
- ❏ ✓ Odd Grammar
- ❏ ✓ Punctuation Mistakes
- ❏ ✓ Spelling Mistakes

Day #1 · Day #2 · Day #3 · Day #4

Assessment #26

Publish

Now it is time to publish your writing. Write your final copy on the lines below.
MAKE SURE it turns out:

- NEAT—Make sure there are no wrinkles, creases, or holes.
- CLEAN—Erase any smudges or dirty spots.
- EASY TO READ—Use your best handwriting and good spacing between words.

_____

_____

_____

_____

_____

_____

_____

_____

_____

_____

_____

_____

_____

_____

_____

_____

_____

_____

Underline with three short lines the first letter of each word that should be capitalized.

1. My sister, irene thompson, lives on white avenue.

Circle the correct verb for the irregular past tense verb.

2. Yesterday, Miguel (draws, drew, has drawn) a dragon with a silver bell.

Add the punctuation. In the blank before the sentence, write **S** (statement), **Q** (question), **C** (command), or **E** (exclamation).

3. _____ Yay, no science test today _____

Fill in the circle beside the word that correctly finishes the sentence.

4. Iggy said, "_____ my best friend."   o Your   o You're

Underline with three short lines the first letter of each word that should be capitalized.

1. Sherrie went to seattle to visit aunt Diane and uncle rob for the weekend.

Circle the correct verb for the irregular past tense verb.

2. I hope the sunflower seed (grows, grew, has grown) tonight so I can see its sprout in the morning.

Add the punctuation. In the blank before the sentence, write **S** (statement), **Q** (question), **C** (command), or **E** (exclamation).

3. _____ What are we doing instead of the science test _____

Fill in the circle beside the word that correctly finishes the sentence.

4. They are taking _____ spacecraft to the repair shop.   o their   o they're

---

Underline with three short lines the first letter of each word that should be capitalized.

1. They went to the Seattle aquarium and saw gina, the sea otter, and oscar, the octopus.

Circle the correct verb for the irregular past tense verb.

2. Since December, Janet (sang, has sung) every Saturday with the choir.

Add the punctuation. In the blank before the sentence, write **S** (statement), **Q** (question), **C** (command), or **E** (exclamation).

3. _____ We are doing a magnet experiment _____

Fill in the circle beside the word that correctly finishes the sentence.

4. The repairman told Iggy _____ beyond repair.   o its   o it's

---

Underline with three short lines the first letter of each word that should be capitalized.

1. They ate lunch at neptune Café and then they drove to yeager Airport.

Circle the correct verb for the irregular past tense verb.

2. I (write, wrote, have written) a letter to my grandpa last week.

Add the punctuation. In the blank before the sentence, write **S** (statement), **Q** (question), **C** (command), or **E** (exclamation).

3. _____ Go get the magnets for our group, please _____

Fill in the circle beside the word that correctly finishes the sentence.

4. I think _____ going to have to buy a new spacecraft.   o your   o you're

Day #1

Day #2

Day #3

Day #4

Assessment # 27

Underline with three short lines the first letter of each word that should be capitalized.

1. My grandmother went to college at The art Institute, while Grandpa jones worked at the indianapolis Zoo.

2. After graduating, grandma became the art teacher at south academy High School.

Circle the correct verb for the irregular past tense verb.

3. My father (drives, drove, has driven) three thousand miles since he got his new truck.

4. I (see, saw, have seen) a funny television program last night.

5. Barney (thinks, thought, has thought) he wants to be an astronaut when he grows up.

Add the punctuation. In the blank before each sentence, write **S** (statement), **Q** (question), **C** (command), or **E** (exclamation).

6. _____ Mario, check if there are horseshoe magnets _____

7. _____ Oh, no _____

8. _____ I spilled the magnets _____

Fill in the circle beside the word that correctly finishes each sentence.

9. _____ going shopping tomorrow.

     ◯ Their   ◯ They're

10. Iggy and Wiggy will use the money for _____ new spacecraft.

     ◯ their   ◯ they're

prewrite/brainstorm

Continue your narrative writing. You and your best friend are at the beach on Saturday, and you find a bottle with a treasure map inside. Look at the second event you created, and write a list of words that describe and explain the event.

_____	_____	_____
_____	_____	_____
_____	_____	_____

draft

Write a descriptive paragraph about the second event that happened after you found the treasure map.

_____

_____

_____

_____

_____

revise

Read your paragraph. Does it have a topic sentence? Does it have points that fit your topic sentence? Rewrite your paragraph, and make your words more specific.

_____

_____

_____

_____

_____

proofread

Now it's time to proofread your paragraph describing the second event. Are all of the words spelled correctly? Did you capitalize words that need to be capitalized? Did you use the correct verbs and nouns? Proofread your paragraph.

- ❑ ✓ Capitalization Mistakes
- ❑ ✓ Odd Grammar
- ❑ ✓ Punctuation Mistakes
- ❑ ✓ Spelling Mistakes

Day #1
Day #2
Day #3
Day #4

Assessment

Assessment #28

Publish

Now it is time to publish your writing. Write your final copy on the lines below.

MAKE SURE it turns out:

- NEAT—Make sure there are no wrinkles, creases, or holes.
- CLEAN—Erase any smudges or dirty spots.
- EASY TO READ—Use your best handwriting and good spacing between words.

_____

_____

_____

_____

_____

_____

_____

_____

_____

_____

_____

_____

_____

_____

_____

_____

_____

_____

_____

_____

Write your favorite(s) for each category. Remember to capitalize proper nouns.

1. person _____ animal _____ color _____

Circle the nouns in the sentence.

2. The Great Lakes are five big lakes in the Midwest.

Correct the punctuation and spelling mistakes in the boxes below.

3.

| Mickey Mouses hole | Tues | May 8 | 6 pm. |

Write a sentence using the corrected information from the boxes.

4. _____

Write your favorite(s) for each category. Remember to capitalize proper nouns.

1. food _____ school subject _____ sport or game _____

Circle the nouns in the sentence.

2. The Great Lakes have shores made up of sand, rocks, cliffs, and hills.

Correct the punctuation and spelling mistakes in the boxes below.

3.

| Spidermans' house | Fri | Jan 12 | 3 pm |

Write a sentence using the corrected information from the boxes.

4. _____

Write your favorite(s) for each category. Remember to capitalize proper nouns.

1. place _____ city _____ state _____

Circle the nouns in the sentence.

2. Visitors can see many birds that live there.

Correct the punctuation and spelling mistakes in the boxes below.

3.

| Scrooges' office | Mon. | Feb 2 | 4 p.m. |

Write a sentence using the corrected information from the boxes.

4. _____

Write your favorite(s) for each category. Remember to capitalize proper nouns.

1. artist _____ author _____ book _____

Circle the nouns in the sentence.

2. Birds that live near the Great Lakes are sea gulls, ducks, geese, sandpipers, and eagles.

Correct the punctuation and spelling mistakes in the boxes below.

3.

| Wonder Womans jet | Wed | May 12 | 8 pm |

Write a sentence using the corrected information from the boxes.

4. _____

Assessment

Assessment #29

Write your favorite(s) for each category. Remember to capitalize the first letter of words that are proper nouns.

1. book _____

   song _____

   movie _____

2. poem _____

   singer or group _____

   TV program _____

Circle the nouns in the sentences.

3. Many people live along the Great Lakes.

4. Fishermen work on their boats on the lakes.

5. Men and women run stores, hotels, and restaurants.

6. Visitors like the beaches and the water.

Correct the punctuation and spelling mistakes in the boxes below. Then write a sentence using the corrected information from each set of boxes.

7.

| Cinderellas castle | Thurs | Oct 5 | 9 am. |

8. _____

   _____

9.

| Stuart Littles' house | Sat | May 23 | 5 pm |

10. _____

   _____

prewrite/brainstorm

Now it's time to write your conclusion to the narrative about finding the treasure map. Make a list of ideas you want to include in your resolution to the problem.

_____

_____

_____

_____

_____

Day #1

draft

Look over your list. What are the important items you want to say in your conclusion? Write a paragraph based on those items.

_____

_____

_____

_____

_____

Day #2

revise

Read over your conclusion paragraph. Does it have a topic sentence? Does it have a concluding sentence? Did you leave anything out? Did you put in too much description? Rewrite your paragraph to make it more specific.

_____

_____

_____

_____

_____

Day #3

proofread

Proofread your conclusion paragraph that resolves your problem. Are all of the words spelled correctly? Did you capitalize words that need to be capitalized? Did you use the correct verbs and nouns? Make proofreading marks in your paragraph.

- ❏ ✓ Capitalization Mistakes
- ❏ ✓ Odd Grammar
- ❏ ✓ Punctuation Mistakes
- ❏ ✓ Spelling Mistakes

Day #4

Assessment #30

Publish

Now it is time to publish your writing. Write your final copy on the lines below.

MAKE SURE it turns out:

- NEAT—Make sure there are no wrinkles, creases, or holes.
- CLEAN—Erase any smudges or dirty spots.
- EASY TO READ—Use your best handwriting and good spacing between words.

_____

_____

_____

_____

_____

_____

_____

_____

_____

_____

_____

_____

_____

_____

_____

_____

_____

_____

_____

_____

Name

Underline with three short lines the first letter of each word that should be capitalized.

1. r. j. smith moved to the north end of meadow avenue.

Read the sentence. Then rewrite the sentence correctly, using the proper past-tense irregular verb.

2. Wrong: My sister breaked my mom's watch.

Correct: _____

Add the correct punctuation.

3. Mr. Weise is Kaci's father He is a musician in New York.

Write the correct plural nouns.

4. There were six (turkey) _____ and two (goose) _____ in the petting zoo.

Day #1

Underline with three short lines the first letter of each word that should be capitalized.

1. my friend's dog, annabell, had puppies on march 4, 1998.

Read the sentence. Then rewrite the sentence correctly, using the proper past-tense irregular verb.

2. Wrong: I catched the ball.

Correct: _____

Add the correct punctuation.

3. Kaci's mother an engineer travels a lot.

Write the correct plural nouns.

4. We bought a bouquet of (daisy) _____ and some (peach) _____ at the market.

Day #2

Underline with three short lines the first letter of each word that should be capitalized.

1. when my uncle, dr. kenneth johnson, visited us on thanksgiving day, we sang songs.

Read the sentence. Then rewrite the sentence correctly, using the proper past-tense irregular verb.

2. Wrong: I was so thirsty that I drinked the whole glass of water.

Correct: _____

Add the correct punctuation.

3. We went to a football game Our team won!

Write the correct plural nouns.

4. Three (shelf) _____ in the china cabinet held water (glass) _____ .

Day #3

Underline with three short lines the first letter of each word that should be capitalized.

1. did nora and irene join the girl scouts of america last january?

Read the sentence. Then rewrite the sentence correctly, using the proper past-tense irregular verb.

2. Wrong: My class readed 145 books for the reading contest.

Correct: _____

Add the correct punctuation.

3. In Chicago we watched a baseball game.

Write the correct plural nouns.

4. Four (man) _____ chased seven (deer) _____ through the forest.

Day #4

Assessment #31

Underline with three short lines the first letter of each word that should be capitalized.

1. while in france, aunt rachel learned to make fine french pastry.

2. elizabeth's grandmother, who lives in the east, collects native american pottery.

Read the sentences. Then rewrite the sentences correctly, using the proper past-tense irregular verb.

3. Wrong: We swimmed in my aunt's pool all day.

    Correct: _____

4. Wrong: Mom, Leslie taked my dinosaur.

    Correct: _____

5. Wrong: My grandpa teached me how to ride a bike.

    Correct: _____

Add the correct punctuation.

6. The Rio Grande in the United States goes through three states The three states are Colorado, New Mexico, and Texas The river starts in Colorado.

7. The Rio Grande is a natural border between Texas and Mexico You can see it on a map It is one of the most interesting rivers in the United States.

Write the correct plural nouns to complete the sentence.

8. Jenny was one of five (child) _____ in her family to go to these (university) _____.

9. We traveled to two big (city) _____ and saw three famous (museum) _____.

10. Those (cow) _____ gave birth to seven (calf) _____ all together.

prewrite/brainstorm

Poetry tells about feelings, ideas, or events. Write a poem about your favorite time of year. Start your poem by first writing your favorite time of year in the box below. Next, make a list of all the ideas that you think of about that time of year.

_____   _____

_____   _____

_____   _____

draft

Look at your list of ideas about your favorite time of year. Pick out three ideas that are most important. Now write a rough draft of your poem based on these ideas. Can you make the lines rhyme?

_____

_____

_____

_____

revise

Read your poem about your favorite time of year. Can you make your nouns and verbs more specific? Can you make the last words of each couplet, which is a pair of lines, rhyme with each other? Rewrite the poem and make it more specific.

_____

_____

_____

_____

proofread

It's time to proofread your poem. Are all of the words spelled correctly? Did you capitalize words that need to be capitalized? Did you use the correct verbs and nouns? Make proofreading marks in your poem.

- ❑ ✓ Capitalization Mistakes
- ❑ ✓ Odd Grammar
- ❑ ✓ Punctuation Mistakes
- ❑ ✓ Spelling Mistakes

Assessment #32

Publish

Now it is time to publish your writing. Write your final copy on the lines below.

MAKE SURE it turns out:

- NEAT—Make sure there are no wrinkles, creases, or holes.
- CLEAN—Erase any smudges or dirty spots.
- EASY TO READ—Use your best handwriting and good spacing between words.

Underline with three short lines the first letter of each word that should be capitalized.

1. Are you looking for a copy of *treasure island*?

If the boldfaced verb is used incorrectly, write the proper verb on the line.

2. Many parents and relatives had **came** to see the children perform. _____

Read the sentence. Then add the missing commas.

3. Wendy Wesley and William are washing Wilma Winkel's windows.

Circle the correct homophone to complete the sentence.

4. The (great/grate) kept the leaves out of the drain.

Underline with three short lines the first letter of each word that should be capitalized.

1. Do you want to read *the lorax*?

If the boldfaced verb is used incorrectly, write the proper verb on the line.

2. The show **began** with the fifth-grade band. _____

Read the sentence. Then add the missing commas.

3. Silly Sally sat on a steeple sipping soda sewing shirts and singing spooky songs.

Circle the correct homophone to complete the sentence.

4. I feel (great/grate) today because I passed the test.

Underline with three short lines the first letter of each word that should be capitalized.

1. come in to Booker's book Shop. we promise to have the book you want.

If the boldfaced verb is used incorrectly, write the proper verb on the line.

2. Hector recited a poem he had **wrote**. _____

Read the sentence. Then add the missing commas.

3. Last night, Lannie Lily and Larry licked lollipops while buying lemons licorice and lettuce at Lucky's.

Circle the correct homophone to complete the sentence.

4. He decided to (weight/wait).

Underline with three short lines the first letter of each word that should be capitalized.

1. There is only one great bookstore in north America, and it's ours!

If the boldfaced verb is used incorrectly, write the proper verb on the line.

2. I **done** several magic tricks. _____

Read the sentence. Then add the missing commas.

3. Big Bill Boone Bonnie Bell and Barry Burke baked bread while bouncing blue basketballs.

Circle the correct homophone to complete the sentence.

4. You have gained so much (weight/wait)!

Assessment #33

Assessment

Underline with three short lines the first letter of each word that should be capitalized.

1. Mr. kahn said, "there is no book shop like booker's."

2. at Booker's, we will keep you reading.

If the boldfaced verb is used incorrectly, write the proper verb on the line.

3. I got so nervous that I **bited** my tongue. _____

4. I almost **forgotten** to put my rabbit in my hat. _____

5. They had **driven** across country to watch her perform. _____

Read the sentence. Then add the missing commas.

6. Yesterday, handsome Harry hung a hammock played the harmonica and hit a homerun.

7. Jonathan Julie Jacob and Joseph are juggling jugs and jumping rope.

8. Miss Mary Moore makes many mini muffins milks cows and mends mittens.

Circle the correct homophone to complete the sentence.

9. It is supposed to (rein/rain) tonight.

10. When you ride a horse, remember to hold the (reins/rains).

Day #1

prewrite/brainstorm

A paragraph that tells how things are the same or different is called a compare-and-contrast paragraph. Use the Venn diagram to show how two things are the same or different. Write more ideas about how snakes and dogs are the same or different in the ovals.

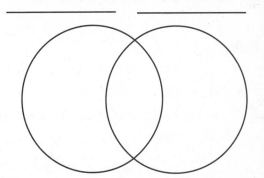

Day #2

draft

Use the information you wrote in the Venn diagram to write a compare-and-contrast paragraph about snakes and dogs.

_____

_____

_____

_____

_____

Day #3

revise

Look at the paragraph you wrote comparing and contrasting dogs and snakes. Did you begin with a topic sentence? Did you use specific words to describe the things that are the same and different about dogs and snakes? Did you use a conclusion sentence? Rewrite your paragraph.

_____

_____

_____

_____

Day #4

proofread

Finally, proofread your compare-and-contrast paragraph. Are all of the words spelled correctly? Did you capitalize words that need to be capitalized? Did you use the correct verbs and nouns? Make proofreading marks in your paragraph.

- ❑ ✓ Capitalization Mistakes
- ❑ ✓ Odd Grammar
- ❑ ✓ Punctuation Mistakes
- ❑ ✓ Spelling Mistakes

Assessment

Assessment #34

Publish

Now it is time to publish your writing. Write your final copy on the lines below.

MAKE SURE it turns out:

- NEAT—Make sure there are no wrinkles, creases, or holes.
- CLEAN—Erase any smudges or dirty spots.
- EASY TO READ—Use your best handwriting and good spacing between words.

_____

_____

_____

_____

_____

_____

_____

_____

_____

_____

_____

_____

_____

_____

_____

_____

_____

_____

_____

_____

                       0-7682-3224-4 *Write 4 Today*

Name

Underline with three short lines the first letter of each word that should be capitalized in the title.

1. Have you read *stuart little*? It's a book about a mouse.

Fill in the circle next to the correct verb.

2. You will feel better if you _____ down.   o lay   o lie

Underline the title of the book or movie.

3. They have made the book The Wizard of Oz into a movie.

Draw a delete mark through the incorrect word and write the correct word in the blank.

4. There are four gooses in the pond. _____

Underline with three short lines the first letter of each word that should be capitalized in the title.

1. The song "row, row, row your boat" is fun to sing.

Fill in the circle next to the correct verb.

2. _____ the books on the table.   o Lay   o Lie

Underline the title of the book or movie.

3. A book I'd like to read is The Iron Giant by Ted Hughes.

Draw a delete mark through the incorrect word and write the correct word in the blank.

4. Jody's uncle raises oxes on his ranch. _____

Underline with three short lines the first letter of each word that should be capitalized in the title.

1. I saw the play *the sound of music*.

Fill in the circle next to the correct verb.

2. The chickens will not _____ any eggs.   o lay   o lie

Underline the title of the book or movie.

3. Two DVDs I'd like to see are Shrek and The Muppet Movie.

Draw a delete mark through the incorrect word and write the correct word in the blank.

4. Jody and her brother-in-laws help take care of the crops. _____

Underline with three short lines the first letter of each word that should be capitalized in the title.

1. We always watch *sesame street*.

Fill in the circle next to the correct verb.

2. I told my dog to _____ down on the porch.   o lay   o lie

Underline the title of the book or movie.

3. That book is called Bridge to Terabithia.

Draw a delete mark through the incorrect word and write the correct word in the blank.

4. The flys bothered the horses and other farm animals. _____

Assessment #35

Underline with three short lines the first letter of each word that should be capitalized in the title.

1. Kari read *harriet the spy* to her sister.

2. One of my favorite books is *Little house on the prairie* by Laura Ingalls Wilder.

3. C. S. Lewis wrote a book called *The lion, the witch, and the wardrobe.*

Fill in the circle next to the correct verb.

4. My hamster _____ in his nest all day.

    ○ lays

    ○ lies

5. My teacher _____ her papers on the desk.

    ○ lays

    ○ lies

6. The cat _____ in the flowerbed.

    ○ lays

    ○ lies

Underline the title of the book or movie.

7. I think the movie Holes is really good.

8. Do you like the book Mary Poppins?

Draw a delete mark through the incorrect word and write the correct word in the blank.

9. Large groupes watched the dolphins perform every half hour. _____

10. Modeles of mammals were exhibited at the aquarium. _____

prewrite/brainstorm

When writing, don't tell the reader what he or she should see. Show the reader. Use specific words to create a picture for the reader. Read the sentence. It doesn't show the reader the day; it just tells about the day. On the lines, list reasons it was a nice day.

It was a nice day.

draft

Look over your list of reasons it was a nice day. Now, write a paragraph describing the nice day. Be sure to include a topic sentence and a concluding sentence.

revise

Does your paragraph about a nice day have a topic sentence? Does it have a concluding sentence? Did you leave anything out? Did you put in too much description? Rewrite your paragraph to make it more specific.

proofread

Finally, proofread your paragraph. Are all of the words spelled correctly? Did you capitalize words that need to be capitalized? Did you use the correct verbs and nouns? Make proofreading marks in your paragraph.

- ❐ ✓ Capitalization Mistakes
- ❐ ✓ Odd Grammar
- ❐ ✓ Punctuation Mistakes
- ❐ ✓ Spelling Mistakes

Assessment #36

Publish

Now it is time to publish your writing. Write your final copy on the lines below.
MAKE SURE it turns out:

- NEAT—Make sure there are no wrinkles, creases, or holes.
- CLEAN—Erase any smudges or dirty spots.
- EASY TO READ—Use your best handwriting and good spacing between words.

_____

_____

_____

_____

_____

_____

_____

_____

_____

_____

_____

_____

_____

_____

_____

_____

_____

_____

Circle the first letter of each word that has a capitalization mistake in the title.

1. Have you read *Tales Of A Fourth Grade Nothing* by Judy Blume?

Fill in the circle that correctly completes the sentence.

2. Mr. Nguyen is a _____ music teacher. O good   O well

Insert a comma to correct this compound sentence.

3. The only wild one-hump camels in the world are now found in australia yet these animals were first brought to australia in 1840.

Draw a delete mark through the misspelled words. Write the correct spelling above them.

4. **Gum-Everlasting** – Does your gum loose its flavor? Dose it gets hard after only twelve hours?

Circle the first letter of each word that has a capitalization mistake in the title.

1. My sister didn't like the book *Chicken Soup With Rice* by Maurice Sendak.

Fill in the circle that correctly completes the sentence.

2. Matthew plays tennis _____. O badly   O bad

Insert a comma to correct this compound sentence.

3. Alligators have broad, flat, rounded snouts but crocodiles have longer, sharper snouts.

Draw a delete mark through the misspelled words. Write the correct spelling above them.

4. You need too try new Gum-Everlasting! Why? Yule get all-day chewing enjoyment!

Circle the first letter of each word that has a capitalization mistake in the title.

1. A movie with good songs is *The Sound Of Music*.

Fill in the circle that correctly completes the sentence.

2. Ricardo is the _____ volleyball player on our team. O best   O worse

Insert a comma to correct this compound sentence.

3. The Anteater has a coarse gray coat with white-bordered stripes on each shoulder and its tail is long and Bushy.

Draw a delete mark through the misspelled words. Write the correct spelling above them.

4. You'll also get our new, high-tech Gum Reflaviator. Put you're old gum inside the Reflaviator before you go to bed.

Circle the first letter of each word that has a capitalization mistake in the title.

1. The song "All I Want For Christmas Is My Two Front Teeth" makes me laugh.

Fill in the circle that correctly completes the sentence.

2. Justin played _____ on Monday than Tuesday. O gooder   O better

Insert a comma to correct this compound sentence.

3. Giraffes must spread their long forelegs widely to reach the ground so they rarely Graze on grass.

Draw a delete mark through the misspelled words. Write the correct spelling above them.

4. When you get up in the morning, your gum is sotf, flavorful, and ready for another day. So, buy your Gum-Everlasting today!

Day #1

Day #2

Day #3

Day #4

Assessment # 37

Circle the first letter of each word that has a capitalization mistake in the title.

1. Have you read the book *Little House In The Big Woods*?

2. I want to see the play *The Man Who Loved To Laugh*.

3. My favorite television program is *Where In The World Is Carmen Sandiego*?

Fill in the circle that correctly completes the sentence.

4. Kara snowboards even _____ than Hayley.

   ○ worse   ○ worser

5. Anne dances very _____.

   ○ good   ○ well

6. Jenna's team played _____ last night.

   ○ bad   ○ badly

Use the conjunction in parethesis to write a compound sentence.

7. Penguins walk or hop and toboggan along on their breasts, pushing with wings and feet. They swim with great speed and agility. (or)

   _____

   _____

8. Many endangered species live in the rain forest. People around the world are working to preserve their habitat. (but)

   _____

   _____

Draw a delete mark through the misspelled words and write the correct spelling above them.

9. Brother-Be-Gone! Chessa had a big problem—her brothers. When she goed to her room to play with her friends, her brothers allways followed them.

10. Thay teased Chessa and laught at her. Then Chessa tryed Brother-Be-Gone.

0-7682-3224-4 *Write 4 Today*

Assessment

Name

prewrite/brainstorm

Read the topic sentences below. Circle one that you would like to write about. Next, think about specific details that will support or bolster your topic sentence. Make a list of your ideas.

Main Idea	Details
• Forgetting to do my homework is not a good thing!	_____
• My bike helmet will never, ever be left home again!	_____
• Pizza is the most delicious food ever!	_____
• Saturday is the best day of the week!	_____

Day #1

draft

Using the list you created for your topic sentence, write one paragraph about your topic. You can change the topic sentence slightly, if you want. For example, instead of writing, "Pizza is the most delicious food ever!" you could write, "Tacos are the most delicious food ever!"

_____

_____

_____

_____

Day #2

revise

Does your paragraph support your topic sentence? Does it have a concluding sentence? Did you leave anything out? Did you put in too much description? Rewrite your paragraph to make it more specific.

_____

_____

_____

_____

Day #3

proofread

Proofread your paragraph. Are all of the words spelled correctly? Did you capitalize words that need to be capitalized? Did you use the correct verbs and nouns? Make proofreading marks in your paragraph.

- ❑ ✓ Capitalization Mistakes
- ❑ ✓ Odd Grammar
- ❑ ✓ Punctuation Mistakes
- ❑ ✓ Spelling Mistakes

Day #4

Assessment #38

Publish

Now it is time to publish your writing. Write your final copy on the lines below.
MAKE SURE it turns out:

- NEAT—Make sure there are no wrinkles, creases, or holes.
- CLEAN—Erase any smudges or dirty spots.
- EASY TO READ—Use your best handwriting and good spacing between words.

_____

_____

_____

_____

_____

_____

_____

_____

_____

_____

_____

_____

_____

_____

_____

_____

_____

_____

_____

_____

Use the proper proofreading marks to correct the sentences below.

1. Today my class went on a field trip to the denver Museum of natural History. we saw an exhibit called "remember the Children: Daniel's Story."

Write the correct pronoun to complete the sentence.

2. _____ (I, me) have always wanted to go snorkeling.

Fill in the circle next to the words and punctuation that correctly complete the sentence.

3. & 4.   Daniel bought two _____ of bread and a sack of _____ for lunch _____ he loves food.
   - O loafs
   - O loafes
   - O loaves
   - O potatoies
   - O potatos
   - O potatoes
   - O . he
   - O ; he
   - O , He

Use the proper proofreading marks to correct the sentences below.

1. The exhibit was about a Jewish boy who grew up in germany in the 1930s and survived the Holocaust. daniel was not a real boy, but his story was based on real events.

Write the correct pronoun to complete the sentence.

2. My friend, Freddie, is going to teach _____ (I, me) how to snorkel this weekend.

Fill in the circle next to the words and punctuation that correctly complete the sentence.

3. & 4.   There were several _____ and hundreds of _____ at the park _____ it was beautiful.
   - O gooses
   - O geese
   - O geeses
   - O butterflies
   - O butterflyes
   - O butterflys
   - O ; it
   - O , It
   - O . it

Use the proper proofreading marks to correct the sentences below.

1. The exhibit had a display of a typical german home. It also showed a part titled "scary Changes." This part showed how the nazi Party made unfair rules for Jewish people.

Write the correct pronoun to complete the sentence.

2. _____ (He, Him) has been snorkeling for many years.

Fill in the circle next to the words and punctuation that correctly complete the sentence.

3. & 4.   Ten _____ were sitting on the _____ of the tree _____ they were looking at me!
   - O monkieys
   - O monkeys
   - O monkeyes
   - O branchs
   - O branches
   - O branchies
   - O ; they
   - O , They
   - O . they

Use the proper proofreading marks to correct the sentences below.

1. another part of the exhibit was "The ghetto." Daniel's family and other jewish families were forced to move into a small section of another city.

Write the correct pronoun to complete the sentence.

2. Freddie's grandfather taught _____ (he, him) how to snorkel.

Fill in the circle next to the words and punctuation that correctly complete the sentence.

3. & 4.   Those _____ have broken _____ in their cars _____ they need new ones.
   - O men
   - O mans
   - O mens
   - O stereos
   - O stereoes
   - O stereoies
   - O , They
   - O . they
   - O ; they

Assessment #39

Use the proper proofreading marks to correct the sentences below.

1. The past part of the exhibit was titled "the concentration Camp." Many Jewish people were killed there, but not Daniel.

2. at the end of the exhibit, the museum had volunteers who talked with us about what we saw.

3. Even though it was not a fun trip, i am glad we went. we learned a lot about the holocaust.

Write the correct pronoun to complete the sentence.

4. _____ (We, Us) are going to his favorite spot where the coral is beautiful.

5. _____ (He, Him) told _____ (I, me) to rent a mask, fins, and snorkel at

Snorkel Bob's.

6. Snorkel Bob asked Freddie and _____ (I, me) if _____ (us, we) had been

snorkeling before.

Fill in the circle next to the words and punctuation that correctly complete the sentences.

7. & 8.   The _____ were terrified _____ they saw 10 _____ scurry across the floor.

    ◯ ladies   ◯ , They   ◯ mices

    ◯ ladyes   ◯ ; they   ◯ mouses

    ◯ ladys   ◯ . they   ◯ mice

9. & 10.   The _____ in the closet were filled with _____ and toys _____ they were stuffed.

    ◯ shelfs   ◯ clothies   ◯ , They

    ◯ shelfes   ◯ clothes   ◯ . they

    ◯ shelves   ◯ clothyes   ◯ ; they

Name

Day #1

prewrite/brainstorm

News stories contain facts and answer the questions who? what? where? when? why? and how? Read the paragraph. Make a list of facts that answer these questions.

The Ghost Town of Calico: Founded in 1881. About $85 million in silver was mined from Calico. Calico once had 22 saloons. Walter Knott, a former miner, bought Calico and brought some of its buildings to another California town. There, he created Knott's Berry Farm. Then he fixed up the other buildings in Calico and made that a tourist attraction. He added some new "old" buildings, too. You can also see a pretend gunfight, a museum, people dressed in clothes from the 1800s, and a Civil War re-enactment.

draft

Write a news story paragraph that answers the five Ws and H about the ghost town of Calico. Use your list to help to organize the paragraph.

_____

_____

_____

_____

_____

Day #2

revise

Look at your paragraph. Does it have a topic sentence? Does it have a concluding sentence? Did you leave any information out? Rewrite your paragraph to make it more specific.

_____

_____

_____

_____

_____

Day #3

proofread

Finally, proofread your paragraph. Are all of the words spelled correctly? Did you capitalize words that need to be capitalized? Did you use the correct verbs and nouns? Make proofreading marks in your paragraph.

- ☐ ✓ Capitalization Mistakes
- ☐ ✓ Odd Grammar
- ☐ ✓ Punctuation Mistakes
- ☐ ✓ Spelling Mistakes

Day #4

Assessment # 40

Assessment

Publish

Now it is time to publish your writing. Write your final copy on the lines below.

MAKE SURE it turns out:

- NEAT—Make sure there are no wrinkles, creases, or holes.
- CLEAN—Erase any smudges or dirty spots.
- EASY TO READ—Use your best handwriting and good spacing between words.

_____

_____

_____

_____

_____

_____

_____

_____

_____

_____

_____

_____

_____

_____

_____

_____

_____

_____

_____

_____

Answer Key

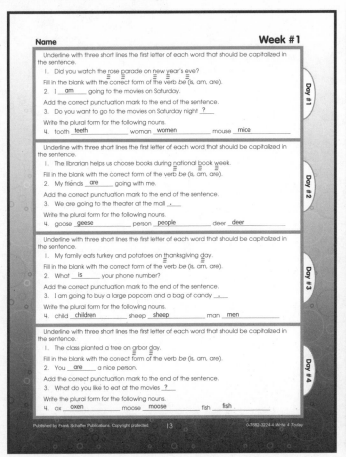

Day #1

Underline with three short lines the first letter of each word that should be capitalized in the sentence.
1. Did you watch the rose parade on new year's eve?
Fill in the blank with the correct form of the verb *be* (is, am, are).
2. I __am__ going to the movies on Saturday.
Add the correct punctuation mark to the end of the sentence.
3. Do you want to go to the movies on Saturday night _?_
Write the plural form for the following nouns.
4. tooth __teeth__   woman __women__   mouse __mice__

Day #2

Underline with three short lines the first letter of each word that should be capitalized in the sentence.
1. The librarian helps us choose books during national book week.
Fill in the blank with the correct form of the verb *be* (is, am, are).
2. My friends __are__ going with me.
Add the correct punctuation mark to the end of the sentence.
3. We are going to the theater at the mall _._
Write the plural form for the following nouns.
4. goose __geese__   person __people__   deer __deer__

Day #3

Underline with three short lines the first letter of each word that should be capitalized in the sentence.
1. My family eats turkey and potatoes on thanksgiving day.
Fill in the blank with the correct form of the verb *be* (is, am, are).
2. What __is__ your phone number?
Add the correct punctuation mark to the end of the sentence.
3. I am going to buy a large popcorn and a bag of candy _._
Write the plural form for the following nouns.
4. child __children__   sheep __sheep__   man __men__

Day #4

Underline with three short lines the first letter of each word that should be capitalized in the sentence.
1. The class planted a tree on arbor day.
Fill in the blank with the correct form of the verb *be* (is, am, are).
2. You __are__ a nice person.
Add the correct punctuation mark to the end of the sentence.
3. What do you like to eat at the movies _?_
Write the plural form for the following nouns.
4. ox __oxen__   moose __moose__   fish __fish__

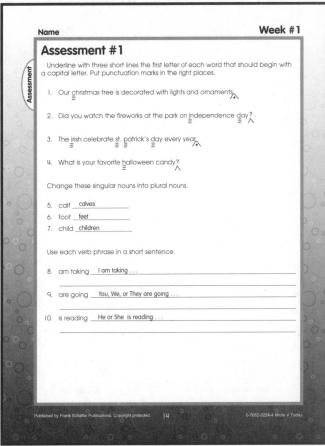

Assessment #1

Underline with three short lines the first letter of each word that should begin with a capital letter. Put punctuation marks in the right places.

1. Our christmas tree is decorated with lights and ornaments.
2. Did you watch the fireworks at the park on independence day?
3. The irish celebrate st. patrick's day every year.
4. What is your favorite halloween candy?

Change these singular nouns into plural nouns.

5. calf __calves__
6. foot __feet__
7. child __children__

Use each verb phrase in a short sentence.

8. am taking __I am taking . . .__
9. are going __You, We, or They are going . . .__
10. is reading __He or She is reading . . .__

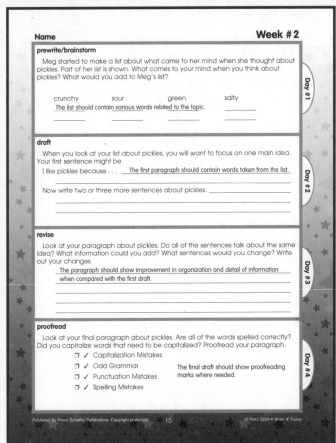

Day #1

prewrite/brainstorm

Meg started to make a list about what came to her mind when she thought about pickles. Part of her list is shown. What comes to your mind when you think about pickles? What would you add to Meg's list?

crunchy   sour   green   salty
__The list should contain various words related to the topic.__

Day #2

draft

When you look at your list about pickles, you will want to focus on one main idea. Your first sentence might be

I like pickles because . . . __The first paragraph should contain words taken from the list.__

Now write two or three more sentences about pickles. _____

Day #3

revise

Look at your paragraph about pickles. Do all of the sentences talk about the same idea? What information could you add? What sentences would you change? Write out your changes.

__The paragraph should show improvement in organization and detail of information when compared with the first draft.__

Day #4

proofread

Look at your final paragraph about pickles. Are all of the words spelled correctly? Did you capitalize words that need to be capitalized? Proofread your paragraph.

☐ ✓ Capitalization Mistakes
☐ ✓ Odd Grammar
☐ ✓ Punctuation Mistakes   The final draft should show proofreading marks where needed.
☐ ✓ Spelling Mistakes

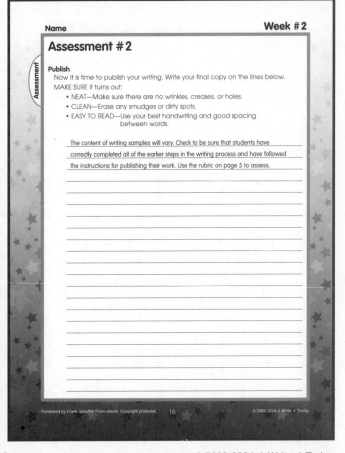

Assessment #2

Publish

Now it is time to publish your writing. Write your final copy on the lines below. MAKE SURE it turns out:
- NEAT—Make sure there are no wrinkles, creases, or holes.
- CLEAN—Erase any smudges or dirty spots.
- EASY TO READ—Use your best handwriting and good spacing between words.

__The content of writing samples will vary. Check to be sure that students have correctly completed all of the earlier steps in the writing process and have followed the instructions for publishing their work. Use the rubric on page 5 to assess.__

Answer Key

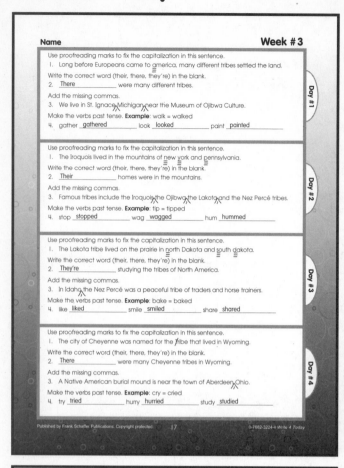

Use proofreading marks to fix the capitalization in this sentence.
1. Long before Europeans came to america, many different tribes settled the land.
Write the correct word (their, there, they're) in the blank.
2. There were many different tribes.
Add the missing commas.
3. We live in St. Ignace Michigan near the Museum of Ojibwa Culture.
Make the verbs past tense. **Example**: walk = walked
4. gather _gathered_   look _looked_   paint _painted_

Day #1

Use proofreading marks to fix the capitalization in this sentence.
1. The Iroquois lived in the mountains of new york and pennsylvania.
Write the correct word (their, there, they're) in the blank.
2. Their homes were in the mountains.
Add the missing commas.
3. Famous tribes include the Iroquois the Ojibwa the Lakota and the Nez Percé tribes.
Make the verbs past tense. **Example**: tip = tipped
4. stop _stopped_   wag _wagged_   hum _hummed_

Day #2

Use proofreading marks to fix the capitalization in this sentence.
1. The Lakota tribe lived on the prairie in north Dakota and south dakota.
Write the correct word (their, there, they're) in the blank.
2. They're studying the tribes of North America.
Add the missing commas.
3. In Idaho the Nez Percé was a peaceful tribe of traders and horse trainers.
Make the verbs past tense. **Example**: bake = baked
4. like _liked_   smile _smiled_   share _shared_

Day #3

Use proofreading marks to fix the capitalization in this sentence.
1. The city of Cheyenne was named for the Tribe that lived in Wyoming.
Write the correct word (their, there, they're) in the blank.
2. There were many Cheyenne tribes in Wyoming.
Add the missing commas.
3. A Native American burial mound is near the town of Aberdeen Ohio.
Make the verbs past tense. **Example**: cry = cried
4. try _tried_   hurry _hurried_   study _studied_

Day #4

   17   0-7682-3224-4 *Write 4 Today*

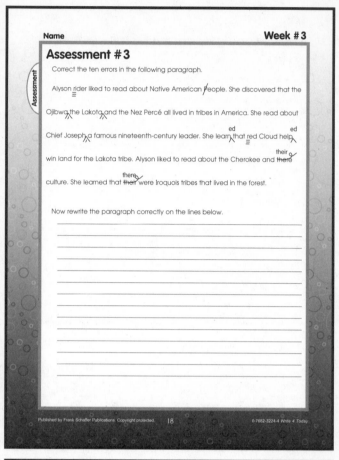

Assessment

Assessment #3

Correct the ten errors in the following paragraph.

Alyson rider liked to read about Native American People. She discovered that the Ojibwa the Lakota and the Nez Percé all lived in tribes in America. She read about Chief Joseph a famous nineteenth-century leader. She learn that red Cloud help win land for the Lakota tribe. Alyson liked to read about the Cherokee and there culture. She learned that their were Iroquois tribes that lived in the forest.

Now rewrite the paragraph correctly on the lines below.

_____
_____
_____
_____
_____
_____
_____
_____
_____
_____
_____
_____

   18   0-7682-3224-4 *Write 4 Today*

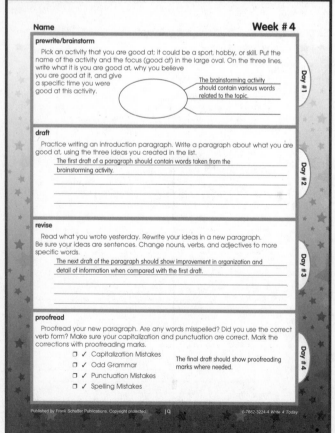

prewrite/brainstorm

Pick an activity that you are good at; it could be a sport, hobby, or skill. Put the name of the activity and the focus (good at) in the large oval. On the three lines, write what it is you are good at, why you believe you are good at it, and give a specific time you were good at this activity.

The brainstorming activity should contain various words related to the topic.

Day #1

draft

Practice writing an introduction paragraph. Write a paragraph about what you are good at, using the three ideas you created in the list.

The first draft of a paragraph should contain words taken from the brainstorming activity.

Day #2

revise

Read what you wrote yesterday. Rewrite your ideas in a new paragraph. Be sure your ideas are sentences. Change nouns, verbs, and adjectives to more specific words.

The next draft of the paragraph should show improvement in organization and detail of information when compared with the first draft.

Day #3

proofread

Proofread your new paragraph. Are any words misspelled? Did you use the correct verb form? Make sure your capitalization and punctuation are correct. Mark the corrections with proofreading marks.

☐ ✓ Capitalization Mistakes
☐ ✓ Odd Grammar
☐ ✓ Punctuation Mistakes
☐ ✓ Spelling Mistakes

The final draft should show proofreading marks where needed.

Day #4

   19   0-7682-3224-4 *Write 4 Today*

Assessment

Assessment #4

Publish

Now it is time to publish your writing. Write your final copy on the lines below. MAKE SURE it turns out:
- NEAT—Make sure there are no wrinkles, creases, or holes.
- CLEAN—Erase any smudges or dirty spots.
- EASY TO READ—Use your best handwriting and good spacing between words.

The content of writing samples will vary. Check to be sure that students have correctly completed all of the earlier steps in the writing process and have followed the instructions for publishing their work. Use the rubric on page 5 to assess.

_____
_____
_____
_____
_____
_____
_____
_____
_____
_____
_____
_____
_____
_____
_____

   20   0-7682-3224-4 *Write 4 Today*

Answer Key

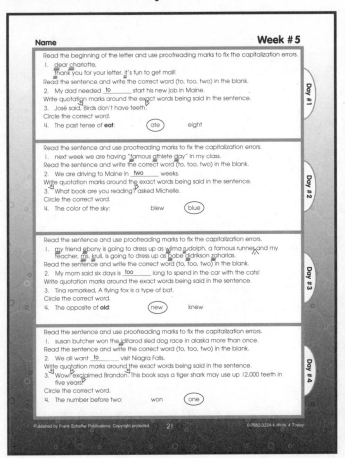

Name

Read the beginning of the letter and use proofreading marks to fix the capitalization errors.
1. dear charlotte,
   thank you for your letter. it's fun to get mail!
Read the sentence and write the correct word (to, too, two) in the blank.
2. My dad needed _to_ start his new job in Maine.
Write quotation marks around the exact words being said in the sentence.
3. José said, Birds don't have teeth.
Circle the correct word.
4. The past tense of **eat**:   (ate)   eight

Day #1

Read the sentence and use proofreading marks to fix the capitalization errors.
1. next week we are having "famous athlete day" in my class.
Read the sentence and write the correct word (to, too, two) in the blank.
2. We are driving to Maine in _two_ weeks.
Write quotation marks around the exact words being said in the sentence.
3. What book are you reading? asked Michelle.
Circle the correct word.
4. The color of the sky: blew   (blue)

Day #2

Read the sentence and use proofreading marks to fix the capitalization errors.
1. my friend ebony is going to dress up as wilma rudolph, a famous runner, and my teacher, ms. krull, is going to dress up as babe didrikson zaharias.
Read the sentence and write the correct word (to, too, two) in the blank.
2. My mom said six days is _too_ long to spend in the car with the cats!
Write quotation marks around the exact words being said in the sentence.
3. Tina remarked, A flying fox is a type of bat.
Circle the correct word.
4. The opposite of **old**:   (new)   knew

Day #3

Read the sentence and use proofreading marks to fix the capitalization errors.
1. susan butcher won the iditarod sled dog race in alaska more than once.
Read the sentence and write the correct word (to, too, two) in the blank.
2. We all want _to_ visit Niagra Falls.
Write quotation marks around the exact words being said in the sentence.
3. Wow! exclaimed Brandon. This book says a tiger shark may use up 12,000 teeth in five years.
Circle the correct word.
4. The number before two: won   (one)

Day #4

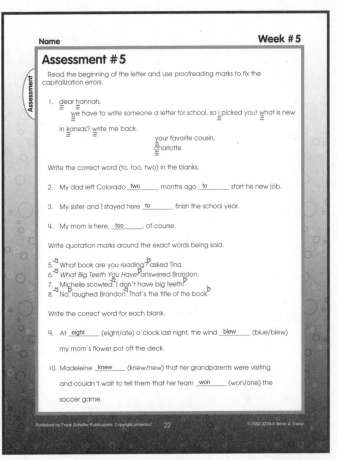

Name

Assessment

Assessment #5

Read the beginning of the letter and use proofreading marks to fix the capitalization errors.

1. dear hannah,
   we have to write someone a letter for school, so i picked you! what is new in kansas? write me back.

   your favorite cousin,
   charlotte

Write the correct word (to, too, two) in the blanks.

2. My dad left Colorado _two_ months ago _to_ start his new job.

3. My sister and I stayed here _to_ finish the school year.

4. My mom is here, _too_, of course.

Write quotation marks around the exact words being said.

5. What book are you reading? asked Tina.
6. What Big Teeth You Have answered Brandon.
7. Michelle scowled. I don't have big teeth!
8. No, laughed Brandon. That's the title of the book.

Write the correct word for each blank.

9. At _eight_ (eight/ate) o'clock last night, the wind _blew_ (blue/blew) my mom's flower pot off the deck.

10. Madeleine _knew_ (knew/new) that her grandparents were visiting and couldn't wait to tell them that her team _won_ (won/one) the soccer game.

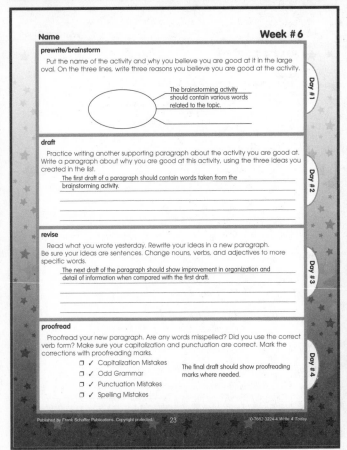

Name

prewrite/brainstorm
   Put the name of the activity and why you believe you are good at it in the large oval. On the three lines, write three reasons you believe you are good at the activity.

The brainstorming activity should contain various words related to the topic.

Day #1

draft
   Practice writing another supporting paragraph about the activity you are good at. Write a paragraph about why you are good at this activity, using the three ideas you created in the list.

The first draft of a paragraph should contain words taken from the brainstorming activity.

Day #2

revise
   Read what you wrote yesterday. Rewrite your ideas in a new paragraph. Be sure your ideas are sentences. Change nouns, verbs, and adjectives to more specific words.

The next draft of the paragraph should show improvement in organization and detail of information when compared with the first draft.

Day #3

proofread
   Proofread your new paragraph. Are any words misspelled? Did you use the correct verb form? Make sure your capitalization and punctuation are correct. Mark the corrections with proofreading marks.
   ☐ ✓ Capitalization Mistakes
   ☐ ✓ Odd Grammar   The final draft should show proofreading
   ☐ ✓ Punctuation Mistakes   marks where needed.
   ☐ ✓ Spelling Mistakes

Day #4

Name

Assessment

Assessment #6

Publish
Now it is time to publish your writing. Write your final copy on the lines below.
MAKE SURE it turns out:
   • NEAT—Make sure there are no wrinkles, creases, or holes.
   • CLEAN—Erase any smudges or dirty spots.
   • EASY TO READ—Use your best handwriting and good spacing between words.

The content of writing samples will vary. Check to be sure that students have correctly completed all of the earlier steps in the writing process and have followed the instructions for publishing their work. Use the rubric on page 5 to assess.

Answer Key

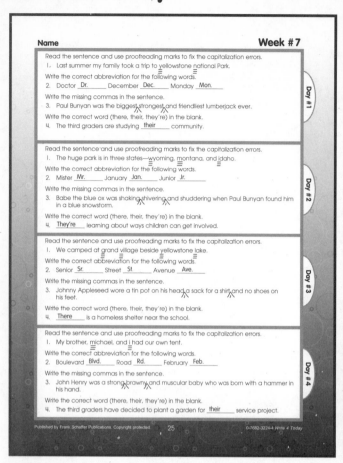

Day #1

Read the sentence and use proofreading marks to fix the capitalization errors.

1. Last summer my family took a trip to yellowstone national Park.

Write the correct abbreviation for the following words.

2. Doctor _Dr._   December _Dec._   Monday _Mon._

Write the missing commas in the sentence.

3. Paul Bunyan was the biggest strongest and friendliest lumberjack ever.

Write the correct word (there, their, they're) in the blank.

4. The third graders are studying _their_ community.

Day #2

Read the sentence and use proofreading marks to fix the capitalization errors.

1. The huge park is in three states—wyoming, montana, and idaho.

Write the correct abbreviation for the following words.

2. Mister _Mr._   January _Jan._   Junior _Jr._

Write the missing commas in the sentence.

3. Babe the blue ox was shaking shivering and shuddering when Paul Bunyan found him in a blue snowstorm.

Write the correct word (there, their, they're) in the blank.

4. _They're_ learning about ways children can get involved.

Day #3

Read the sentence and use proofreading marks to fix the capitalization errors.

1. We camped at grand village beside yellowstone lake.

Write the correct abbreviation for the following words.

2. Senior _Sr._   Street _St._   Avenue _Ave._

Write the missing commas in the sentence.

3. Johnny Appleseed wore a tin pot on his head a sack for a shirt and no shoes on his feet.

Write the correct word (there, their, they're) in the blank.

4. _There_ is a homeless shelter near the school.

Day #4

Read the sentence and use proofreading marks to fix the capitalization errors.

1. My brother, michael, and i had our own tent.

Write the correct abbreviation for the following words.

2. Boulevard _Blvd._   Road _Rd._   February _Feb._

Write the missing commas in the sentence.

3. John Henry was a strong brawny and muscular baby who was born with a hammer in his hand.

Write the correct word (there, their, they're) in the blank.

4. The third graders have decided to plant a garden for _their_ service project.

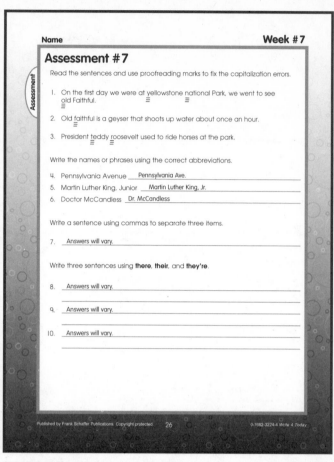

Assessment

Assessment #7

Read the sentences and use proofreading marks to fix the capitalization errors.

1. On the first day we were at yellowstone national Park, we went to see old Faithful.

2. Old faithful is a geyser that shoots up water about once an hour.

3. President teddy roosevelt used to ride horses at the park.

Write the names or phrases using the correct abbreviations.

4. Pennsylvania Avenue _Pennsylvania Ave._

5. Martin Luther King, Junior _Martin Luther King, Jr._

6. Doctor McCandless _Dr. McCandless_

Write a sentence using commas to separate three items.

7. _Answers will vary._

Write three sentences using **there**, **their**, and **they're**.

8. _Answers will vary._

9. _Answers will vary._

10. _Answers will vary._

---

prewrite/brainstorm

Day #1

Put the name of the activity you are good at in the large oval. Write your three main ideas from your supporting paragraphs on the three lines.

The brainstorming activity should contain various words related to the topic.

draft

Day #2

Practice writing a concluding paragraph that sums up, or summarizes, the information you wrote about the activity you are good at. Use the three ideas you created in the list.

The first draft of a paragraph should contain words taken from the brainstorming activity.

revise

Day #3

Read what you wrote yesterday. Rewrite your ideas in a new paragraph. Be sure your ideas are sentences. Change nouns, verbs, and adjectives to more specific words.

The next draft of the paragraph should show improvement in organization and detail of information when compared with the first draft.

proofread

Day #4

Proofread your new paragraph. Are any words misspelled? Did you use the correct verb form? Make sure your capitalization and punctuation are correct. Mark the corrections with proofreading marks.

- ☐ ✓ Capitalization Mistakes
- ☐ ✓ Odd Grammar
- ☐ ✓ Punctuation Mistakes
- ☐ ✓ Spelling Mistakes

The final draft should show proofreading marks where needed.

Put all of the paragraphs together and see your five-paragraph writing!

Assessment

Assessment #8

Publish

Now it is time to publish your writing. Write your final copy on the lines below. MAKE SURE it turns out:

- NEAT—Make sure there are no wrinkles, creases, or holes.
- CLEAN—Erase any smudges or dirty spots.
- EASY TO READ—Use your best handwriting and good spacing between words.

The content of writing samples will vary. Check to be sure that students have correctly completed all of the earlier steps in the writing process and have followed the instructions for publishing their work. Use the rubric on page 5 to assess.

Answer Key

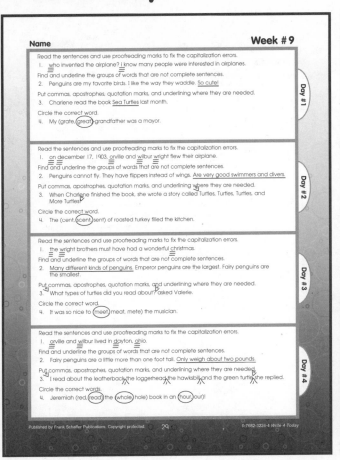

Read the sentences and use proofreading marks to fix the capitalization errors.
1. who invented the airplane? I know many people were interested in airplanes.
Find and underline the groups of words that are not complete sentences.
2. Penguins are my favorite birds. I like the way they waddle. So cute!
Put commas, apostrophes, quotation marks, and underlining where they are needed.
3. Charlene read the book Sea Turtles last month.
Circle the correct word.
4. My (grate, great) grandfather was a mayor.

Day #1

Read the sentences and use proofreading marks to fix the capitalization errors.
1. on december 17, 1903, orville and wilbur wright flew their airplane.
Find and underline the groups of words that are not complete sentences.
2. Penguins cannot fly. They have flippers instead of wings. Are very good swimmers and divers.
Put commas, apostrophes, quotation marks, and underlining where they are needed.
3. When Charlene finished the book, she wrote a story called Turtles, Turtles, Turtles, and More Turtles.
Circle the correct word.
4. The (cent, scent, sent) of roasted turkey filled the kitchen.

Day #2

Read the sentences and use proofreading marks to fix the capitalization errors.
1. the wright brothers must have had a wonderful christmas.
Find and underline the groups of words that are not complete sentences.
2. Many different kinds of penguins. Emperor penguins are the largest. Fairy penguins are the smallest.
Put commas, apostrophes, quotation marks, and underlining where they are needed.
3. What types of turtles did you read about? asked Valerie.
Circle the correct word.
4. It was so nice to (meet, meat, mete) the musician.

Day #3

Read the sentences and use proofreading marks to fix the capitalization errors.
1. orville and wilbur lived in dayton, ohio.
Find and underline the groups of words that are not complete sentences.
2. Fairy penguins are a little more than one foot tall. Only weigh about two pounds.
Put commas, apostrophes, quotation marks, and underlining where they are needed.
3. I read about the leatherback, the loggerhead, the hawksbill, and the green turtle, she replied.
Circle the correct words.
4. Jeremiah (red, read) the (whole, hole) book in an (hour, our)!

Day #4

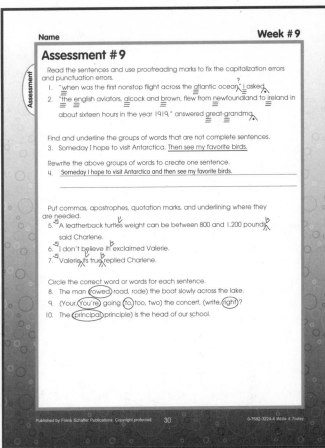

Assessment · **Assessment #9**

Read the sentences and use proofreading marks to fix the capitalization errors and punctuation errors.
1. "when was the first nonstop flight across the atlantic ocean" i asked.
2. "the english aviators, alcock and brown, flew from newfoundland to ireland in about sixteen hours in the year 1919," answered great-grandma.

Find and underline the groups of words that are not complete sentences.
3. Someday I hope to visit Antarctica. Then see my favorite birds.

Rewrite the above groups of words to create one sentence.
Someday I hope to visit Antarctica and then see my favorite birds.

Put commas, apostrophes, quotation marks, and underlining where they are needed.
5. A leatherback turtle's weight can be between 800 and 1,200 pounds, said Charlene.
6. I don't believe it! exclaimed Valerie.
7. Valerie, it's true, replied Charlene.

Circle the correct word or words for each sentence.
8. The man (rowed, road, rode) the boat slowly across the lake.
9. (Your, You're) going (to, too, two) the concert, (write, right)?
10. The (principal, principle) is the head of our school.

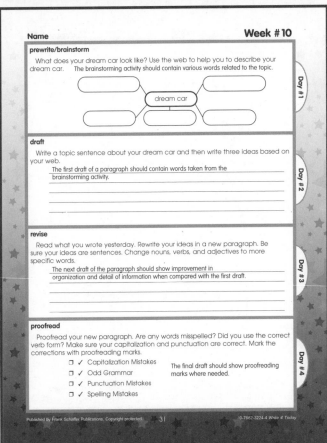

prewrite/brainstorm
What does your dream car look like? Use the web to help you to describe your dream car.   The brainstorming activity should contain various words related to the topic.

dream car

Day #1

draft
Write a topic sentence about your dream car and then write three ideas based on your web.
The first draft of a paragraph should contain words taken from the brainstorming activity.

Day #2

revise
Read what you wrote yesterday. Rewrite your ideas in a new paragraph. Be sure your ideas are sentences. Change nouns, verbs, and adjectives to more specific words.
The next draft of the paragraph should show improvement in organization and detail of information when compared with the first draft.

Day #3

proofread
Proofread your new paragraph. Are any words misspelled? Did you use the correct verb form? Make sure your capitalization and punctuation are correct. Mark the corrections with proofreading marks.
☐ ✓ Capitalization Mistakes
☐ ✓ Odd Grammar   The final draft should show proofreading
☐ ✓ Punctuation Mistakes   marks where needed.
☐ ✓ Spelling Mistakes

Day #4

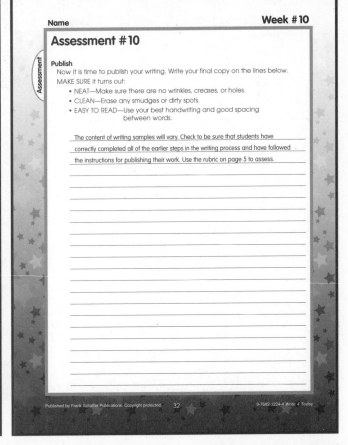

Assessment · **Assessment #10**

Publish
Now it is time to publish your writing. Write your final copy on the lines below.
MAKE SURE it turns out:
• NEAT—Make sure there are no wrinkles, creases, or holes.
• CLEAN—Erase any smudges or dirty spots.
• EASY TO READ—Use your best handwriting and good spacing between words.

The content of writing samples will vary. Check to be sure that students have correctly completed all of the earlier steps in the writing process and have followed the instructions for publishing their work. Use the rubric on page 5 to assess.

Answer Key

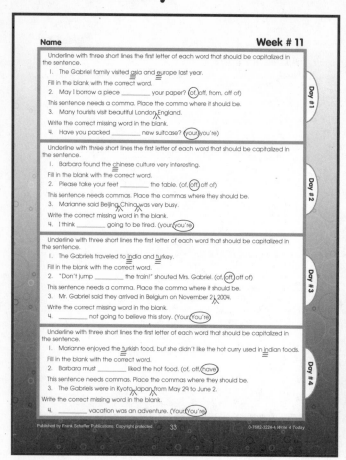

Underline with three short lines the first letter of each word that should be capitalized in the sentence.

1. The Gabriel family visited asia and europe last year.

Fill in the blank with the correct word.

2. May I borrow a piece _____ your paper? (of, off, from, off of)

This sentence needs a comma. Place the comma where it should be.

3. Many tourists visit beautiful London, England.

Write the correct missing word in the blank.

4. Have you packed _____ new suitcase? (your, you're)

Day #1

Underline with three short lines the first letter of each word that should be capitalized in the sentence.

1. Barbara found the chinese culture very interesting.

Fill in the blank with the correct word.

2. Please take your feet _____ the table. (of, off, off of)

This sentence needs commas. Place the commas where they should be.

3. Marianne said Beijing, China, was very busy.

Write the correct missing word in the blank.

4. I think _____ going to be tired. (your, you're)

Day #2

Underline with three short lines the first letter of each word that should be capitalized in the sentence.

1. The Gabriels traveled to india and turkey.

Fill in the blank with the correct word.

2. "Don't jump _____ the train!" shouted Mrs. Gabriel. (of, off, off of)

This sentence needs a comma. Place the comma where it should be.

3. Mr. Gabriel said they arrived in Belgium on November 21, 2004.

Write the correct missing word in the blank.

4. _____ not going to believe this story. (Your, You're)

Day #3

Underline with three short lines the first letter of each word that should be capitalized in the sentence.

1. Marianne enjoyed the turkish food, but she didn't like the hot curry used in indian foods.

Fill in the blank with the correct word.

2. Barbara must _____ liked the hot food. (of, off, have)

This sentence needs commas. Place the commas where they should be.

3. The Gabriels were in Kyoto, Japan, from May 29 to June 2.

Write the correct missing word in the blank.

4. _____ vacation was an adventure. (Your, You're)

Day #4

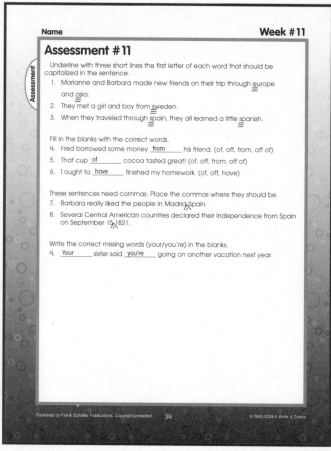

Assessment #11

Assessment

Underline with three short lines the first letter of each word that should be capitalized in the sentence.

1. Marianne and Barbara made new friends on their trip through europe and asia.

2. They met a girl and boy from sweden.

3. When they traveled through spain, they all learned a little spanish.

Fill in the blanks with the correct words.

4. Fred borrowed some money _from___ his friend. (of, off, from, off of)

5. That cup _of___ cocoa tasted great! (of, off, from, off of)

6. I ought to _have___ finished my homework. (of, off, have)

These sentences need commas. Place the commas where they should be.

7. Barbara really liked the people in Madrid, Spain.

8. Several Central American countries declared their independence from Spain on September 15, 1821.

Write the correct missing words (your/you're) in the blanks.

9. _Your___ sister said _you're___ going on another vacation next year.

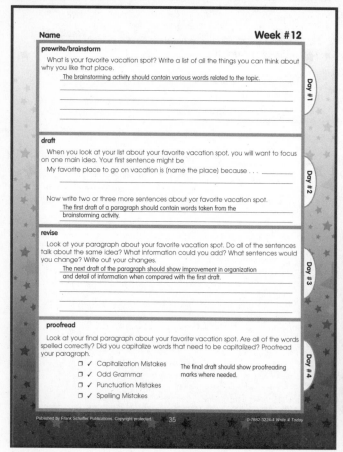

prewrite/brainstorm

What is your favorite vacation spot? Write a list of all the things you can think about why you like that place.

The brainstorming activity should contain various words related to the topic.

Day #1

draft

When you look at your list about your favorite vacation spot, you will want to focus on one main idea. Your first sentence might be

My favorite place to go on vacation is (name the place) because . . . _____

Now write two or three more sentences about your favorite vacation spot.

The first draft of a paragraph should contain words taken from the brainstorming activity.

Day #2

revise

Look at your paragraph about your favorite vacation spot. Do all of the sentences talk about the same idea? What information could you add? What sentences would you change? Write out your changes.

The next draft of the paragraph should show improvement in organization and detail of information when compared with the first draft.

Day #3

proofread

Look at your final paragraph about your favorite vacation spot. Are all of the words spelled correctly? Did you capitalize words that need to be capitalized? Proofread your paragraph.

☐ ✓ Capitalization Mistakes

☐ ✓ Odd Grammar

☐ ✓ Punctuation Mistakes

☐ ✓ Spelling Mistakes

The final draft should show proofreading marks where needed.

Day #4

Assessment #12

Assessment

Publish

Now it is time to publish your writing. Write your final copy on the lines below.

MAKE SURE it turns out:

- NEAT—Make sure there are no wrinkles, creases, or holes.
- CLEAN—Erase any smudges or dirty spots.
- EASY TO READ—Use your best handwriting and good spacing between words.

The content of writing samples will vary. Check to be sure that students have correctly completed all of the earlier steps in the writing process and have followed the instructions for publishing their work. Use the rubric on page 5 to assess.

Answer Key

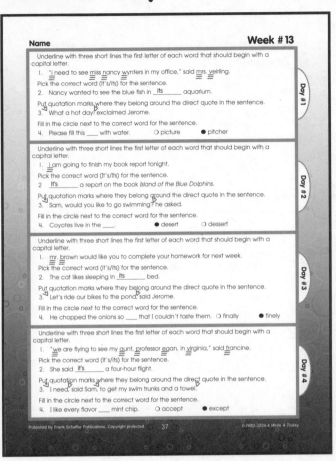

Day #1

Underline with three short lines the first letter of each word that should begin with a capital letter.
1. "i need to see miss nancy wynters in my office," said mrs. veirling.

Pick the correct word (it's/its) for the sentence.
2. Nancy wanted to see the blue fish in ___its___ aquarium.

Put quotation marks where they belong around the direct quote in the sentence.
3. What a hot day! exclaimed Jerome.

Fill in the circle next to the correct word for the sentence.
4. Please fill this ___ with water. ○ picture ● pitcher

Day #2

Underline with three short lines the first letter of each word that should begin with a capital letter.
1. i am going to finish my book report tonight.

Pick the correct word (It's/Its) for the sentence.
2. It's ___ a report on the book Island of the Blue Dolphins.

Put quotation marks where they belong around the direct quote in the sentence.
3. Sam, would you like to go swimming? he asked.

Fill in the circle next to the correct word for the sentence.
4. Coyotes live in the ___. ● desert ○ dessert

Day #3

Underline with three short lines the first letter of each word that should begin with a capital letter.
1. mr. brown would like you to complete your homework for next week.

Pick the correct word (it's/its) for the sentence.
2. The cat likes sleeping in ___its___ bed.

Put quotation marks where they belong around the direct quote in the sentence.
3. Let's ride our bikes to the pond, said Jerome.

Fill in the circle next to the correct word for the sentence.
4. He chopped the onions so ___ that I couldn't taste them. ○ finally ● finely

Day #4

Underline with three short lines the first letter of each word that should begin with a capital letter.
1. "we are flying to see my aunt, professor egan, in virginia," said francine.

Pick the correct word (It's/its) for the sentence.
2. She said ___it's___ a four-hour flight.

Put quotation marks where they belong around the direct quote in the sentence.
3. I need, said Sam, to get my swim trunks and a towel.

Fill in the circle next to the correct word for the sentence.
4. I like every flavor ___ mint chip. ○ accept ● except

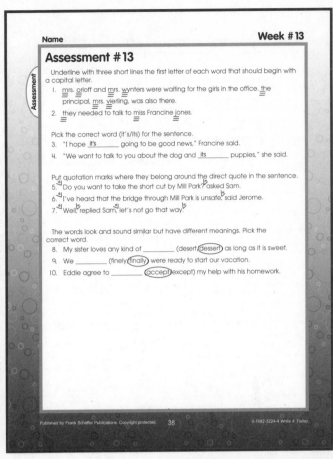

Assessment #13

Underline with three short lines the first letter of each word that should begin with a capital letter.
1. mrs. orloff and mrs. wynters were waiting for the girls in the office. the principal, mrs. vierling, was also there.
2. they needed to talk to miss Francine jones.

Pick the correct word (it's/its) for the sentence.
3. "I hope ___it's___ going to be good news," Francine said.
4. "We want to talk to you about the dog and ___its___ puppies," she said.

Put quotation marks where they belong around the direct quote in the sentence.
5. Do you want to take the short cut by Mill Park? asked Sam.
6. I've heard that the bridge through Mill Park is unsafe, said Jerome.
7. Well, replied Sam, let's not go that way.

The words look and sound similar but have different meanings. Pick the correct word.
8. My sister loves any kind of _____ (desert / (dessert)) as long as it is sweet.
9. We _____ (finely / (finally)) were ready to start our vacation.
10. Eddie agree to _____ ((accept) / except) my help with his homework.

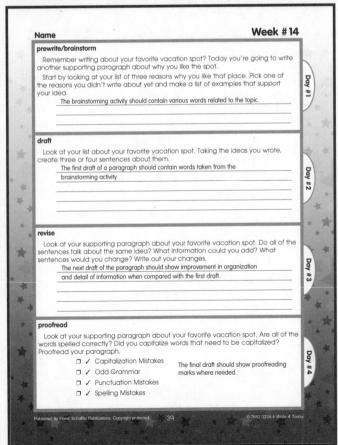

Day #1

prewrite/brainstorm

Remember writing about your favorite vacation spot? Today you're going to write another supporting paragraph about why you like the spot.

Start by looking at your list of three reasons why you like that place. Pick one of the reasons you didn't write about yet and make a list of examples that support your idea.

The brainstorming activity should contain various words related to the topic.

Day #2

draft

Look at your list about your favorite vacation spot. Taking the ideas you wrote, create three or four sentences about them.

The first draft of a paragraph should contain words taken from the brainstorming activity.

Day #3

revise

Look at your supporting paragraph about your favorite vacation spot. Do all of the sentences talk about the same idea? What information could you add? What sentences would you change? Write out your changes.

The next draft of the paragraph should show improvement in organization and detail of information when compared with the first draft.

Day #4

proofread

Look at your supporting paragraph about your favorite vacation spot. Are all of the words spelled correctly? Did you capitalize words that need to be capitalized? Proofread your paragraph.
- ☐ ✓ Capitalization Mistakes
- ☐ ✓ Odd Grammar
- ☐ ✓ Punctuation Mistakes
- ☐ ✓ Spelling Mistakes

The final draft should show proofreading marks where needed.

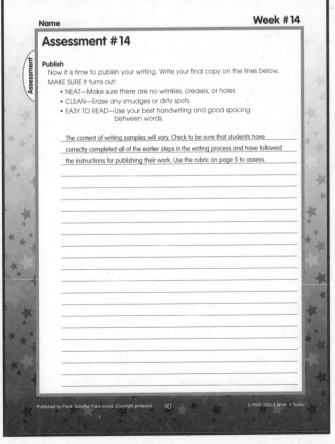

Assessment #14

Publish

Now it is time to publish your writing. Write your final copy on the lines below. MAKE SURE it turns out:
- NEAT—Make sure there are no wrinkles, creases, or holes.
- CLEAN—Erase any smudges or dirty spots.
- EASY TO READ—Use your best handwriting and good spacing between words.

The content of writing samples will vary. Check to be sure that students have correctly completed all of the earlier steps in the writing process and have followed the instructions for publishing their work. Use the rubric on page 5 to assess.

Answer Key

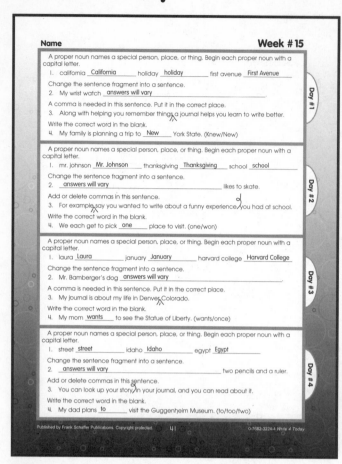

Day #1

A proper noun names a special person, place, or thing. Begin each proper noun with a capital letter.
1. california _California_　holiday _holiday_　first avenue _First Avenue_

Change the sentence fragment into a sentence.
2. My wrist watch _answers will vary_　.

A comma is needed in this sentence. Put it in the correct place.
3. Along with helping you remember things, a journal helps you learn to write better.

Write the correct word in the blank.
4. My family is planning a trip to _New_ York State. (Knew/New)

Day #2

A proper noun names a special person, place, or thing. Begin each proper noun with a capital letter.
1. mr. johnson _Mr. Johnson_　thanksgiving _Thanksgiving_　school _school_

Change the sentence fragment into a sentence.
2. _answers will vary_　likes to skate.

Add or delete commas in this sentence.
3. For example, say you wanted to write about a funny experience you had at school.

Write the correct word in the blank.
4. We each get to pick _one_ place to visit. (one/won)

Day #3

A proper noun names a special person, place, or thing. Begin each proper noun with a capital letter.
1. laura _Laura_　january _January_　harvard college _Harvard College_

Change the sentence fragment into a sentence.
2. Mr. Bamberger's dog _answers will vary_　.

A comma is needed in this sentence. Put it in the correct place.
3. My journal is about my life in Denver, Colorado.

Write the correct word in the blank.
4. My mom _wants_ to see the Statue of Liberty. (wants/once)

Day #4

A proper noun names a special person, place, or thing. Begin each proper noun with a capital letter.
1. street _street_　idaho _Idaho_　egypt _Egypt_

Change the sentence fragment into a sentence.
2. _answers will vary_　two pencils and a ruler.

Add or delete commas in this sentence.
3. You can look up your story in your journal, and you can read about it.

Write the correct word in the blank.
4. My dad plans _to_ visit the Guggenheim Museum. (to/too/two)

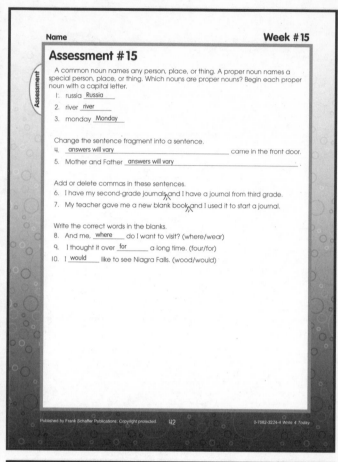

Assessment

Assessment #15

A common noun names any person, place, or thing. A proper noun names a special person, place, or thing. Which nouns are proper nouns? Begin each proper noun with a capital letter.
1. russia _Russia_
2. river _river_
3. monday _Monday_

Change the sentence fragment into a sentence.
4. _answers will vary_　came in the front door.
5. Mother and Father _answers will vary_

Add or delete commas in these sentences.
6. I have my second-grade journals, and I have a journal from third grade.
7. My teacher gave me a new blank book, and I used it to start a journal.

Write the correct words in the blanks.
8. And me, _where_ do I want to visit? (where/wear)
9. I thought it over _for_ a long time. (four/for)
10. I _would_ like to see Niagra Falls. (wood/would)

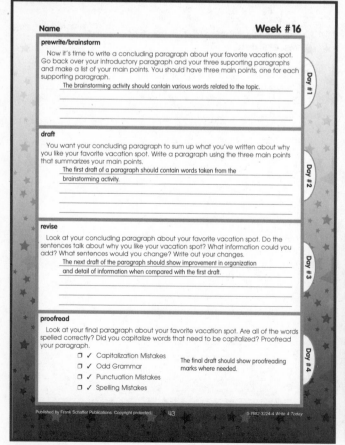

prewrite/brainstorm

Day #1

Now it's time to write a concluding paragraph about your favorite vacation spot. Go back over your introductory paragraph and your three supporting paragraphs and make a list of your main points. You should have three main points, one for each supporting paragraph.
The brainstorming activity should contain various words related to the topic.

draft

Day #2

You want your concluding paragraph to sum up what you've written about why you like your favorite vacation spot. Write a paragraph using the three main points that summarizes your main points.
The first draft of a paragraph should contain words taken from the brainstorming activity.

revise

Day #3

Look at your concluding paragraph about your favorite vacation spot. Do the sentences talk about why you like your vacation spot? What information could you add? What sentences would you change? Write out your changes.
The next draft of the paragraph should show improvement in organization and detail of information when compared with the first draft.

proofread

Day #4

Look at your final paragraph about your favorite vacation spot. Are all of the words spelled correctly? Did you capitalize words that need to be capitalized? Proofread your paragraph.
- ☐ ✓ Capitalization Mistakes
- ☐ ✓ Odd Grammar
- ☐ ✓ Punctuation Mistakes
- ☐ ✓ Spelling Mistakes

The final draft should show proofreading marks where needed.

Assessment

Assessment #16

Publish

Now it is time to publish your writing. Write your final copy on the lines below. MAKE SURE it turns out:
- NEAT—Make sure there are no wrinkles, creases, or holes.
- CLEAN—Erase any smudges or dirty spots.
- EASY TO READ—Use your best handwriting and good spacing between words.

The content of writing samples will vary. Check to be sure that students have correctly completed all of the earlier steps in the writing process and have followed the instructions for publishing their work. Use the rubric on page 5 to assess.

Answer Key

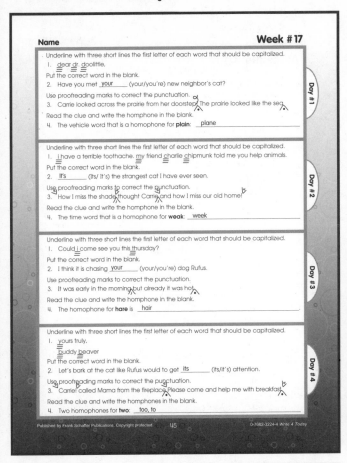

Day #1

Underline with three short lines the first letter of each word that should be capitalized.
1. dear dr. doolittle.

Put the correct word in the blank.
2. Have you met _your_ (your/you're) new neighbor's cat?

Use proofreading marks to correct the punctuation.
3. Carrie looked across the prairie from her doorstep. The prairie looked like the sea.

Read the clue and write the homphone in the blank.
4. The vehicle word that is a homophone for **plain**: _plane_

Day #2

Underline with three short lines the first letter of each word that should be capitalized.
1. i have a terrible toothache. my friend charlie chipmunk told me you help animals.

Put the correct word in the blank.
2. _It's_ (Its/ It's) the strangest cat I have ever seen.

Use proofreading marks to correct the punctuation.
3. How I miss the shade, thought Carrie, and how I miss our old home!

Read the clue and write the homphone in the blank.
4. The time word that is a homophone for **weak**: _week_

Day #3

Underline with three short lines the first letter of each word that should be capitalized.
1. Could i come see you this thursday?

Put the correct word in the blank.
2. I think it is chasing _your_ (your/you're) dog Rufus.

Use proofreading marks to correct the punctuation.
3. It was early in the morning, but already it was hot.

Read the clue and write the homphone in the blank.
4. The homophone for **hare** is _hair_

Day #4

Underline with three short lines the first letter of each word that should be capitalized.
1. yours truly,
   buddy beaver

Put the correct word in the blank.
2. Let's bark at the cat like Rufus would to get _its_ (its/it's) attention.

Use proofreading marks to correct the punctuation.
3. Carrie! called Mama from the fireplace. Please come and help me with breakfast.

Read the clue and write the homphones in the blank.
4. Two homophones for **two**: _too, to_

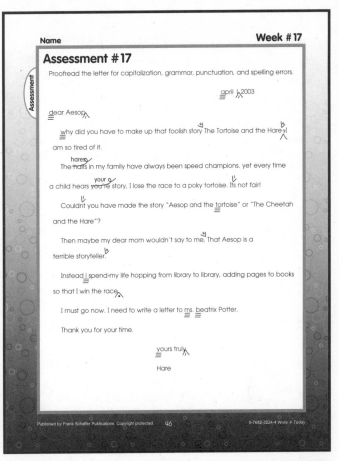

Assessment #17

Proofread the letter for capitalization, grammar, punctuation, and spelling errors.

april 1, 2003

dear Aesop,

why did you have to make up that foolish story The Tortoise and the Hare? I am so tired of it.

The hares in my family have always been speed champions. yet every time a child hears your story, I lose the race to a poky tortoise. It's not fair!

Couldnt you have made the story "Aesop and the tortoise" or "The Cheetah and the Hare"?

Then maybe my dear mom wouldn't say to me, That Aesop is a terrible storyteller.

Instead i spend my life hopping from library to library, adding pages to books so that I win the race.

I must go now. I need to write a letter to ms. beatrix Potter.

Thank you for your time.

yours truly,

Hare

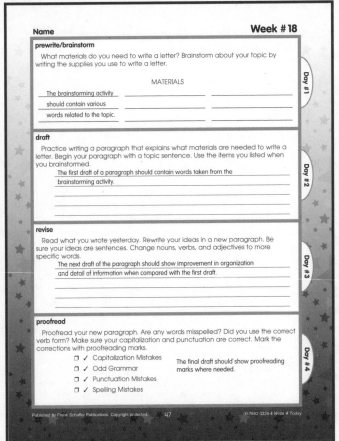

Day #1

prewrite/brainstorm

What materials do you need to write a letter? Brainstorm about your topic by writing the supplies you use to write a letter.

MATERIALS

The brainstorming activity _____ _____
should contain various _____ _____
words related to the topic. _____ _____

Day #2

draft

Practice writing a paragraph that explains what materials are needed to write a letter. Begin your paragraph with a topic sentence. Use the items you listed when you brainstormed.

The first draft of a paragraph should contain words taken from the
brainstorming activity.

Day #3

revise

Read what you wrote yesterday. Rewrite your ideas in a new paragraph. Be sure your ideas are sentences. Change nouns, verbs, and adjectives to more specific words.

The next draft of the paragraph should show improvement in organization
and detail of information when compared with the first draft.

Day #4

proofread

Proofread your new paragraph. Are any words misspelled? Did you use the correct verb form? Make sure your capitalization and punctuation are correct. Mark the corrections with proofreading marks.

☐ ✓ Capitalization Mistakes
☐ ✓ Odd Grammar
☐ ✓ Punctuation Mistakes
☐ ✓ Spelling Mistakes

The final draft should show proofreading
marks where needed.

Assessment #18

Publish

Now it is time to publish your writing. Write your final copy on the lines below.
MAKE SURE it turns out:
- NEAT—Make sure there are no wrinkles, creases, or holes.
- CLEAN—Erase any smudges or dirty spots.
- EASY TO READ—Use your best handwriting and good spacing between words.

The content of writing samples will vary. Check to be sure that students have
correctly completed all of the earlier steps in the writing process and have followed
the instructions for publishing their work. Use the rubric on page 5 to assess.

Answer Key

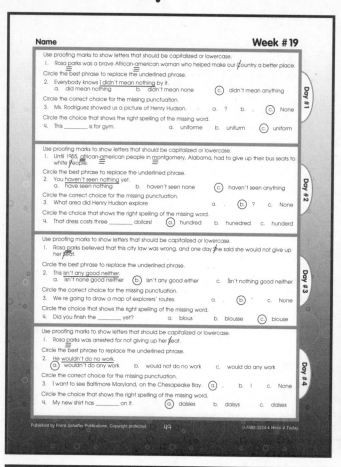

Name

Week #19

Use proofing marks to show letters that should be capitalized or lowercase.
1. Rosa parks was a brave African-american woman who helped make our country a better place.

Circle the best phrase to replace the underlined phrase.
2. Everybody knows I didn't mean nothing by it.
   a. did mean nothing   b. didn't mean none   (c) didn't mean anything

Circle the correct choice for the missing punctuation.
3. Ms. Rodriguez showed us a picture of Henry Hudson.   a. ?   b. .   (c) None

Circle the choice that shows the right spelling of the missing word.
4. This _____ is for gym.   a. uniforme   b. unifurm   (c) uniform

Day #1

Use proofing marks to show letters that should be capitalized or lowercase.
1. Until 1955, african-american people in montgomery, Alabama, had to give up their bus seats to white people.

Circle the best phrase to replace the underlined phrase.
2. You haven't seen nothing yet.
   a. have seen nothing   b. haven't seen none   (c) haven't seen anything

Circle the correct choice for the missing punctuation.
3. What area did Henry Hudson explore   a. .   (b) ?   c. None

Circle the choice that shows the right spelling of the missing word.
4. That dress costs three _____ dollars!   (a) hundred   b. hunedred   c. hunderd

Day #2

Use proofing marks to show letters that should be capitalized or lowercase.
1. Rosa parks believed that this city law was wrong, and one day she said she would not give up her seat.

Circle the best phrase to replace the underlined phrase.
2. This isn't any good neither.
   a. isn't none good neither   (b) isn't any good either   c. isn't nothing good neither

Circle the correct choice for the missing punctuation.
3. We re going to draw a map of explorers' routes.   a. .   (b) '   c. None

Circle the choice that shows the right spelling of the missing word.
4. Did you finish the _____ yet?   a. blous   b. blousse   (c) blouse

Day #3

Use proofing marks to show letters that should be capitalized or lowercase.
1. Rosa parks was arrested for not giving up her seat.

Circle the best phrase to replace the underlined phrase.
2. He wouldn't do no work.
   (a) wouldn't do any work   b. would not do no work   c. would do any work

Circle the correct choice for the missing punctuation.
3. I want to see Baltimore Maryland, on the Chesapeake Bay.   (a) ,   b. .   c. None

Circle the choice that shows the right spelling of the missing word.
4. My new shirt has _____ on it.   (a) daisies   b. daisys   c. daises

Day #4

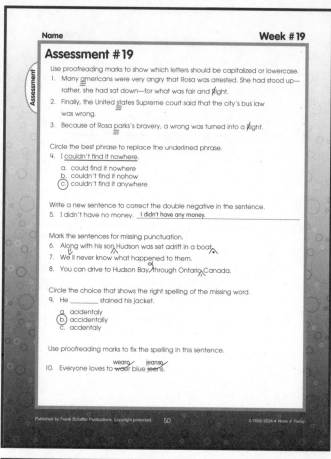

Name

Week #19

Assessment #19

Use proofreading marks to show which letters should be capitalized or lowercase.
1. Many americans were very angry that Rosa was arrested. She had stood up— rather, she had sat down—for what was fair and right.
2. Finally, the United states Supreme court said that the city's bus law was wrong.
3. Because of Rosa parks's bravery, a wrong was turned into a right.

Circle the best phrase to replace the underlined phrase.
4. I couldn't find it nowhere.
   a. could find it nowhere
   b. couldn't find it nohow
   (c) couldn't find it anywhere

Write a new sentence to correct the double negative in the sentence.
5. I didn't have no money.   I didn't have any money.

Mark the sentences for missing punctuation.
6. Along with his son Hudson was set adrift in a boat.
7. We ll never know what happened to them.
8. You can drive to Hudson Bay through Ontario Canada.

Circle the choice that shows the right spelling of the missing word.
9. He _____ stained his jacket.
   a. acidently
   (b) accidentally
   c. acdentaly

Use proofreading marks to fix the spelling in this sentence.
10. Everyone loves to waer blue jeens.

Assessment

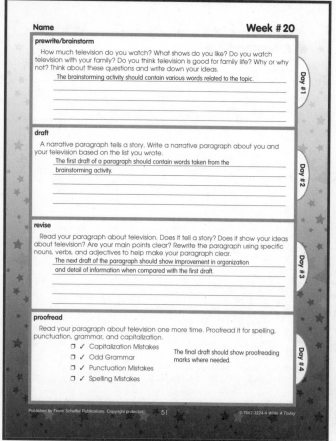

Name

Week #20

prewrite/brainstorm

How much television do you watch? What shows do you like? Do you watch television with your family? Do you think television is good for family life? Why or why not? Think about these questions and write down your ideas.

The brainstorming activity should contain various words related to the topic.

Day #1

draft

A narrative paragraph tells a story. Write a narrative paragraph about you and your television based on the list you wrote.

The first draft of a paragraph should contain words taken from the brainstorming activity.

Day #2

revise

Read your paragraph about television. Does it tell a story? Does it show your ideas about television? Are your main points clear? Rewrite the paragraph using specific nouns, verbs, and adjectives to help make your paragraph clear.

The next draft of the paragraph should show improvement in organization and detail of information when compared with the first draft.

Day #3

proofread

Read your paragraph about television one more time. Proofread it for spelling, punctuation, grammar, and capitalization.

   ☐ ✓ Capitalization Mistakes
   ☐ ✓ Odd Grammar   The final draft should show proofreading
   ☐ ✓ Punctuation Mistakes   marks where needed.
   ☐ ✓ Spelling Mistakes

Day #4

Name

Week #20

Assessment #20

Publish

Now it is time to publish your writing. Write your final copy on the lines below. MAKE SURE it turns out:
   • NEAT—Make sure there are no wrinkles, creases, or holes.
   • CLEAN—Erase any smudges or dirty spots.
   • EASY TO READ—Use your best handwriting and good spacing
      between words.

The content of writing samples will vary. Check to be sure that students have correctly completed all of the earlier steps in the writing process and have followed the instructions for publishing their work. Use the rubric on page 5 to assess.

Assessment

Answer Key

Day #1

Underline with three short lines the first letter of each word that should be capitalized.

1. Morgan Freeman starred in a movie with Jim Carrey called *bruce almighty*.

Underline the predicate in the sentence.

2. Sunshine warms the soil. Then the rain falls.

Add commas where they are needed.

3. Large mammals such as bears, bobcats, and deer live in the Appalachian Mountains.

Put a line through the word that is not spelled correctly. Write the correct spelling in the blank.

4. George Washington Carver was an African-American scintist.   scientist

Day #2

Underline with three short lines the first letter of each word that should be capitalized.

1. Michael Jackson's album *thriller* sold over 45 million copies.

Underline the predicate in the sentence.

2. A seed absorbs water and swells. The swelling splits the seed coat open.

Add commas where they are needed.

3. Pines and junipers grow on the lower slopes of the Rocky Mountains, but firs and spruce grow on the higher areas.

Put a line through the word that is not spelled correctly. Write the correct spelling in the blank.

4. As a boy Carver was always intrested in learning.   interested

Day #3

Underline with three short lines the first letter of each word that should be capitalized.

1. Writer Alice Walker won a Pulitzer Prize for her novel *the color purple*.

Underline the predicate in the sentence.

2. Roots appear and anchor the seed in the soil. Next, a shoot appears.

Add commas where they are needed.

3. Farmers in the Appalachian Mountains grow corn, grow tobacco, and raise poultry.

Put a line through the word that is not spelled correctly. Write the correct spelling in the blank.

4. Carver graduated from colege in 1894 with a degree in agriculture.   college

Day #4

Underline with three short lines the first letter of each word that should be capitalized.

1. W. C. Handy wrote the song "st. louis blues" in 1914.

Underline the predicate in the sentence.

2. The shoot curves upward and pulls the seed leaves with it. Then the shoot straightens.

Add commas where they are needed.

3. Goats and bighorn sheep live in the mountains, but coyotes and moose live in the valleys.

Put a line through the word that is not spelled correctly. Write the correct spelling in the blank.

4. After 1914, he began research on penuts, pecans, and sweet potatoes.   peanuts

---

Assessment   *Assessment # 21*

Underline with three short lines the first letter of each word that should be capitalized.

1. Bill Cosby starred in a television program called *the cosby show* for many years.

2. Maya Angelou wrote a book called *i know why the caged bird sings*.

3. Eddie Murphy starred in *dr. doolittle* and *the nutty professor*.

Underline the predicate in the sentences.

4. The young plant needs water, sunshine, minerals, oxygen, and carbon dioxide to grow well.

5. Minerals come from the soil around the plant's roots.

6. They dissolve in water absorbed by the roots.

Add commas to the following sentences where they are needed.

7. The Appalachian Mountains have rich mineral deposits, important agricultural regions, and recreational areas.

8. The Rocky Mountains run through New Mexico, Colorado, Utah, Wyoming, Idaho, Montana, Washington, and Alaska.

Put a line through the words that are not spelled correctly. Then rewrite the sentence with correct spelling.

9. Carver developed three hundred products from penuts, including face powder, soap, ink, and a milk substatute.

    Carver developed three hundred products from peanuts, including face powder, soap, ink, and a milk substitute.

10. George Washington Carver recieved many awards and honors for his contributions to sciense.

    George Washington Carver received many awards and honors for his contributions to science.

Day #1

prewrite/brainstorm

Pick a room in your home. In the web, put the name of the room in the center circle. In the ovals, write the size, colors, and shapes of the room, its furniture, and any other information you think is important.

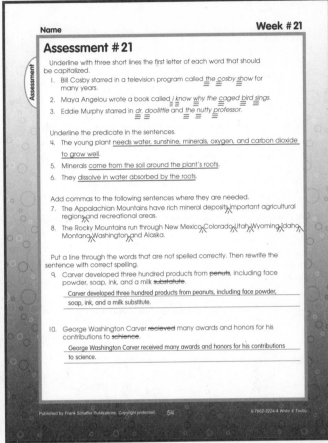

The brainstorming activity should contain various words related to the topic.

Day #2

draft

Practice writing a descriptive paragraph with four or five sentences. Write a paragraph about a room in your house, using the ideas you created in the web.

    The first draft of a paragraph should contain words taken from the brainstorming activity.

Day #3

revise

Read what you wrote about the room. Rewrite your ideas in a new paragraph. Be sure your ideas are sentences. Change nouns, verbs, and adjectives to more specific words.

    The next draft of the paragraph should show improvement in organization and detail of information when compared with the first draft.

Day #4

proofread

Proofread your new paragraph about a room in your home. Are any words misspelled? Did you use the correct verb form? Make sure your capitalization and punctuation are correct. Mark the corrections with proofreading marks.

☐ ✓ Capitalization Mistakes

☐ ✓ Odd Grammar

☐ ✓ Punctuation Mistakes

☐ ✓ Spelling Mistakes

The final draft should show proofreading marks where needed.

Assessment   **Assessment # 22**

Publish

Now it is time to publish your writing. Write your final copy on the lines below. MAKE SURE it turns out:

- NEAT—Make sure there are no wrinkles, creases, or holes.
- CLEAN—Erase any smudges or dirty spots.
- EASY TO READ—Use your best handwriting and good spacing between words.

    The content of writing samples will vary. Check to be sure that students have correctly completed all of the earlier steps in the writing process and have followed the instructions for publishing their work. Use the rubric on page 5 to assess.

Answer Key

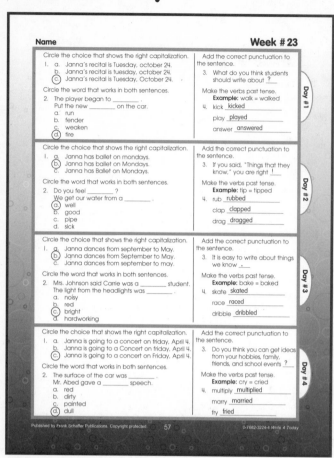

Day #1

Circle the choice that shows the right capitalization.
1. a. Janna's recital is Tuesday, october 24.
   b. Janna's recital is tuesday, october 24.
   c. Janna's recital is Tuesday, October 24.

Circle the word that works in both sentences.
2. The player began to _____.
   Put the new _____ on the car.
   a. run
   b. fender
   c. weaken
   d. tire

Add the correct punctuation to the sentence.
3. What do you think students should write about **?**

Make the verbs past tense.
Example: walk = walked
4. kick _kicked_
   play _played_
   answer _answered_

Day #2

Circle the choice that shows the right capitalization.
1. a. Janna has ballet on mondays.
   b. Janna has ballet on Mondays.
   c. Janna has Ballet on Mondays.

Circle the word that works in both sentences.
2. Do you feel _____?
   We get our water from a _____.
   a. well
   b. good
   c. pipe
   d. sick

Add the correct punctuation to the sentence.
3. If you said, "Things that they know," you are right **!**

Make the verbs past tense.
Example: flip = flipped
4. rub _rubbed_
   clap _clapped_
   drag _dragged_

Day #3

Circle the choice that shows the right capitalization.
1. a. Janna dances from september to May.
   b. Janna dances from September to May.
   c. Janna dances from september to may.

Circle the word that works in both sentences.
2. Mrs. Johnson said Carrie was a _____ student.
   The light from the headlights was _____.
   a. noisy
   b. red
   c. bright
   d. hardworking

Add the correct punctuation to the sentence.
3. It is easy to write about things we know **.**

Make the verbs past tense.
Example: bake = baked
4. skate _skated_
   race _raced_
   dribble _dribbled_

Day #4

Circle the choice that shows the right capitalization.
1. a. Janna is going to a concert on friday, April 4.
   b. Janna is going to a Concert on friday, April 4.
   c. Janna is going to a concert on Friday, April 4.

Circle the word that works in both sentences.
2. The surface of the car was _____.
   Mr. Abed gave a _____ speech.
   a. red
   b. dirty
   c. painted
   d. dull

Add the correct punctuation to the sentence.
3. Do you think you can get ideas from your hobbies, family, friends, and school events **?**

Make the verbs past tense.
Example: cry = cried
4. multiply _multiplied_
   marry _married_
   fry _fried_

Assessment #23

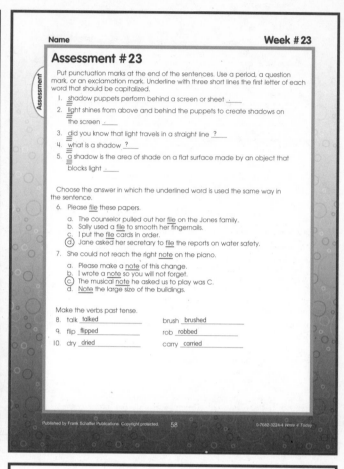

Assessment

Put punctuation marks at the end of the sentences. Use a period, a question mark, or an exclamation mark. Underline with three short lines the first letter of each word that should be capitalized.

1. <u>shadow</u> puppets perform behind a screen or sheet **.**
2. <u>light</u> shines from above and behind the puppets to create shadows on the screen **.**
3. <u>did</u> you know that light travels in a straight line **?**
4. <u>what</u> is a shadow **?**
5. <u>a</u> shadow is the area of shade on a flat surface made by an object that blocks light **.**

Choose the answer in which the underlined word is used the same way in the sentence.

6. Please <u>file</u> these papers.
   a. The counselor pulled out her <u>file</u> on the Jones family.
   b. Sally used a <u>file</u> to smooth her fingernails.
   c. I put the <u>file</u> cards in order.
   d. Jane asked her secretary to <u>file</u> the reports on water safety.

7. She could not reach the right <u>note</u> on the piano.
   a. Please make a <u>note</u> of this change.
   b. I wrote a <u>note</u> so you will not forget.
   c. The musical <u>note</u> he asked us to play was C.
   d. <u>Note</u> the large size of the buildings.

Make the verbs past tense.
8. talk _talked_   brush _brushed_
9. flip _flipped_   rob _robbed_
10. dry _dried_   carry _carried_

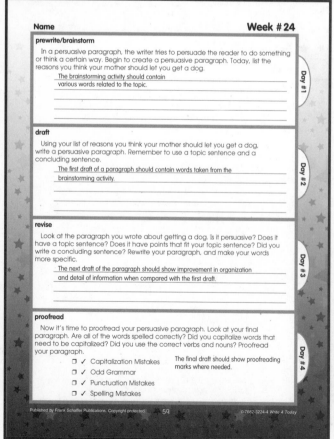

prewrite/brainstorm

In a persuasive paragraph, the writer tries to persuade the reader to do something or think a certain way. Begin to create a persuasive paragraph. Today, list the reasons you think your mother should let you get a dog.

The brainstorming activity should contain various words related to the topic.

Day #1

draft

Using your list of reasons you think your mother should let you get a dog, write a persuasive paragraph. Remember to use a topic sentence and a concluding sentence.

The first draft of a paragraph should contain words taken from the brainstorming activity.

Day #2

revise

Look at the paragraph you wrote about getting a dog. Is it persuasive? Does it have a topic sentence? Does it have points that fit your topic sentence? Did you write a concluding sentence? Rewrite your paragraph, and make your words more specific.

The next draft of the paragraph should show improvement in organization and detail of information when compared with the first draft.

Day #3

proofread

Now it's time to proofread your persuasive paragraph. Look at your final paragraph. Are all of the words spelled correctly? Did you capitalize words that need to be capitalized? Did you use the correct verbs and nouns? Proofread your paragraph.

☐ ✓ Capitalization Mistakes
☐ ✓ Odd Grammar
☐ ✓ Punctuation Mistakes
☐ ✓ Spelling Mistakes

The final draft should show proofreading marks where needed.

Day #4

Assessment #24

Assessment

Publish

Now it is time to publish your writing. Write your final copy on the lines below. MAKE SURE it turns out:

- NEAT—Make sure there are no wrinkles, creases, or holes.
- CLEAN—Erase any smudges or dirty spots.
- EASY TO READ—Use your best handwriting and good spacing between words.

The content of writing samples will vary. Check to be sure that students have correctly completed all of the earlier steps in the writing process and have followed the instructions for publishing their work. Use the rubric on page 5 to assess.

Answer Key

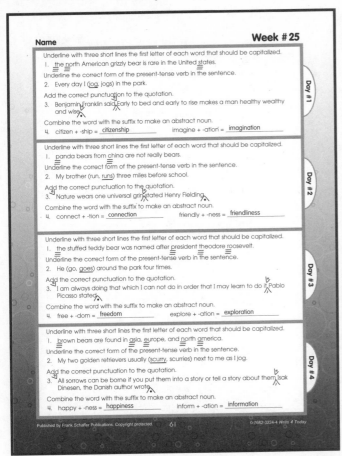

Week # 25

Underline with three short lines the first letter of each word that should be capitalized.
1. the north American grizzly bear is rare in the United states.

Underline the correct form of the present-tense verb in the sentence.
2. Every day I (jog, jogs) in the park.

Add the correct punctuation to the quotation.
3. Benjamin Franklin said Early to bed and early to rise makes a man healthy wealthy and wise

Combine the word with the suffix to make an abstract noun.
4. citizen + -ship = __citizenship__   imagine + -ation = __imagination__

Day #1

Underline with three short lines the first letter of each word that should be capitalized.
1. panda bears from china are not really bears.

Underline the correct form of the present-tense verb in the sentence.
2. My brother (run, runs) three miles before school.

Add the correct punctuation to the quotation.
3. Nature wears one universal grin stated Henry Fielding.

Combine the word with the suffix to make an abstract noun.
4. connect + -tion = __connection__   friendly + -ness = __friendliness__

Day #2

Underline with three short lines the first letter of each word that should be capitalized.
1. the stuffed teddy bear was named after president theodore roosevelt.

Underline the correct form of the present-tense verb in the sentence.
2. He (go, goes) around the park four times.

Add the correct punctuation to the quotation.
3. I am always doing that which I can not do in order that I may learn to do it Pablo Picasso stated

Combine the word with the suffix to make an abstract noun.
4. free + -dom = __freedom__   explore + -ation = __exploration__

Day #3

Underline with three short lines the first letter of each word that should be capitalized.
1. brown bears are found in asia, europe, and north america.

Underline the correct form of the present-tense verb in the sentence.
2. My two golden retrievers usually (scurry, scurries) next to me as I jog.

Add the correct punctuation to the quotation.
3. All sorrows can be borne if you put them into a story or tell a story about them Isak Dinesen, the Danish author wrote

Combine the word with the suffix to make an abstract noun.
4. happy + -ness = __happiness__   inform + -ation = __information__

Day #4

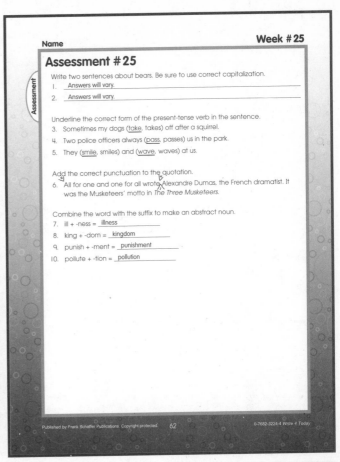

Week # 25

Assessment

Assessment # 25

Write two sentences about bears. Be sure to use correct capitalization.
1. __Answers will vary.__
2. __Answers will vary.__

Underline the correct form of the present-tense verb in the sentence.
3. Sometimes my dogs (take, takes) off after a squirrel.
4. Two police officers always (pass, passes) us in the park.
5. They (smile, smiles) and (wave, waves) at us.

Add the correct punctuation to the quotation.
6. All for one and one for all wrote Alexandre Dumas, the French dramatist. It was the Musketeers' motto in *The Three Musketeers*.

Combine the word with the suffix to make an abstract noun.
7. ill + -ness = __illness__
8. king + -dom = __kingdom__
9. punish + -ment = __punishment__
10. pollute + -tion = __pollution__

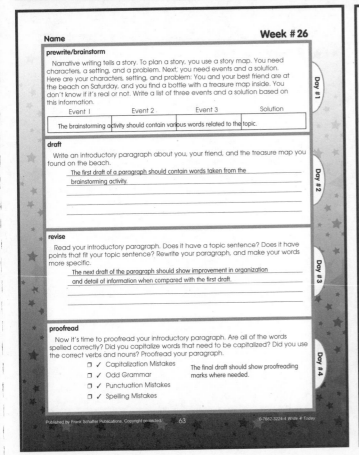

Week # 26

prewrite/brainstorm

Narrative writing tells a story. To plan a story, you use a story map. You need characters, a setting, and a problem. Next, you need events and a solution. Here are your characters, setting, and problem: You and your best friend are at the beach on Saturday, and you find a bottle with a treasure map inside. You don't know if it's real or not. Write a list of three events and a solution based on this information.

Event 1	Event 2	Event 3	Solution
The brainstorming activity should contain various words related to the			topic.

Day #1

draft

Write an introductory paragraph about you, your friend, and the treasure map you found on the beach.

__The first draft of a paragraph should contain words taken from the__
__brainstorming activity.__

Day #2

revise

Read your introductory paragraph. Does it have a topic sentence? Does it have points that fit your topic sentence? Rewrite your paragraph, and make your words more specific.

__The next draft of the paragraph should show improvement in organization__
__and detail of information when compared with the first draft.__

Day #3

proofread

Now it's time to proofread your introductory paragraph. Are all of the words spelled correctly? Did you capitalize words that need to be capitalized? Did you use the correct verbs and nouns? Proofread your paragraph.

☐ ✓ Capitalization Mistakes
☐ ✓ Odd Grammar
☐ ✓ Punctuation Mistakes
☐ ✓ Spelling Mistakes

The final draft should show proofreading marks where needed.

Day #4

Week # 26

Assessment

Assessment # 26

Publish

Now it is time to publish your writing. Write your final copy on the lines below.
MAKE SURE it turns out:
- NEAT—Make sure there are no wrinkles, creases, or holes.
- CLEAN—Erase any smudges or dirty spots.
- EASY TO READ—Use your best handwriting and good spacing between words.

__The content of writing samples will vary. Check to be sure that students have__
__correctly completed all of the earlier steps in the writing process and have followed__
__the instructions for publishing their work. Use the rubric on page 5 to assess.__

Answer Key

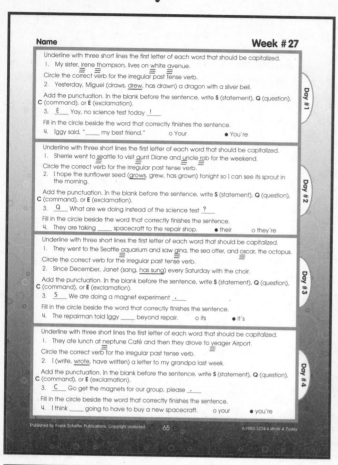

Name — Week # 27

Day #1

Underline with three short lines the first letter of each word that should be capitalized.
1. My sister, irene thompson, lives on white avenue.

Circle the correct verb for the irregular past tense verb.
2. Yesterday, Miguel (draws, <u>drew</u>, has drawn) a dragon with a silver bell.

Add the punctuation. In the blank before the sentence, write **S** (statement), **Q** (question), **C** (command), or **E** (exclamation).
3. _E_ Yay, no science test today _!_

Fill in the circle beside the word that correctly finishes the sentence.
4. Iggy said, "_____ my best friend." ○ Your ● You're

Day #2

Underline with three short lines the first letter of each word that should be capitalized.
1. Sherrie went to seattle to visit aunt Diane and uncle rob for the weekend.

Circle the correct verb for the irregular past tense verb.
2. I hope the sunflower seed (<u>grows</u>, grew, has grown) tonight so I can see its sprout in the morning.

Add the punctuation. In the blank before the sentence, write **S** (statement), **Q** (question), **C** (command), or **E** (exclamation).
3. _Q_ What are we doing instead of the science test _?_

Fill in the circle beside the word that correctly finishes the sentence.
4. They are taking _____ spacecraft to the repair shop. ● their ○ they're

Day #3

Underline with three short lines the first letter of each word that should be capitalized.
1. They went to the Seattle aquarium and saw gina, the sea otter, and oscar, the octopus.

Circle the correct verb for the irregular past tense verb.
2. Since December, Janet (sang, <u>has sung</u>) every Saturday with the choir.

Add the punctuation. In the blank before the sentence, write **S** (statement), **Q** (question), **C** (command), or **E** (exclamation).
3. _S_ We are doing a magnet experiment _._

Fill in the circle beside the word that correctly finishes the sentence.
4. The repairman told Iggy _____ beyond repair. ○ its ● it's

Day #4

Underline with three short lines the first letter of each word that should be capitalized.
1. They ate lunch at neptune Café and then they drove to yeager Airport.

Circle the correct verb for the irregular past tense verb.
2. I (write, <u>wrote</u>, have written) a letter to my grandpa last week.

Add the punctuation. In the blank before the sentence, write **S** (statement), **Q** (question), **C** (command), or **E** (exclamation).
3. _C_ Go get the magnets for our group, please _._

Fill in the circle beside the word that correctly finishes the sentence.
4. I think _____ going to have to buy a new spacecraft. ○ your ● you're

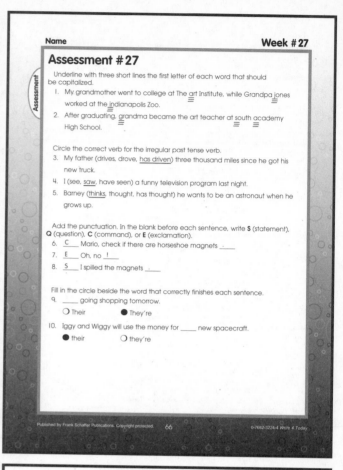

Name — Week # 27

Assessment # 27

Underline with three short lines the first letter of each word that should be capitalized.
1. My grandmother went to college at The art Institute, while Grandpa jones worked at the indianapolis Zoo.
2. After graduating, grandma became the art teacher at south academy High School.

Circle the correct verb for the irregular past tense verb.
3. My father (drives, drove, <u>has driven</u>) three thousand miles since he got his new truck.
4. I (see, <u>saw</u>, have seen) a funny television program last night.
5. Barney (<u>thinks</u>, thought, has thought) he wants to be an astronaut when he grows up.

Add the punctuation. In the blank before each sentence, write **S** (statement), **Q** (question), **C** (command), or **E** (exclamation).
6. _C_ Mario, check if there are horseshoe magnets _._
7. _E_ Oh, no _!_
8. _S_ I spilled the magnets _._

Fill in the circle beside the word that correctly finishes each sentence.
9. _____ going shopping tomorrow.
 ○ Their ● They're
10. Iggy and Wiggy will use the money for _____ new spacecraft.
 ● their ○ they're

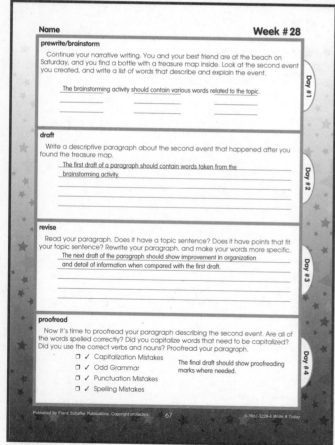

Name — Week # 28

prewrite/brainstorm

Continue your narrative writing. You and your best friend are at the beach on Saturday, and you find a bottle with a treasure map inside. Look at the second event you created, and write a list of words that describe and explain the event.

<u>The brainstorming activity should contain various words related to the topic.</u>

_____ _____ _____
_____ _____ _____

Day #1

draft

Write a descriptive paragraph about the second event that happened after you found the treasure map.

<u>The first draft of a paragraph should contain words taken from the brainstorming activity.</u>

Day #2

revise

Read your paragraph. Does it have a topic sentence? Does it have points that fit your topic sentence? Rewrite your paragraph, and make your words more specific.

<u>The next draft of the paragraph should show improvement in organization and detail of information when compared with the first draft.</u>

Day #3

proofread

Now it's time to proofread your paragraph describing the second event. Are all of the words spelled correctly? Did you capitalize words that need to be capitalized? Did you use the correct verbs and nouns? Proofread your paragraph.

☐ ✓ Capitalization Mistakes
☐ ✓ Odd Grammar
☐ ✓ Punctuation Mistakes
☐ ✓ Spelling Mistakes

The final draft should show proofreading marks where needed.

Day #4

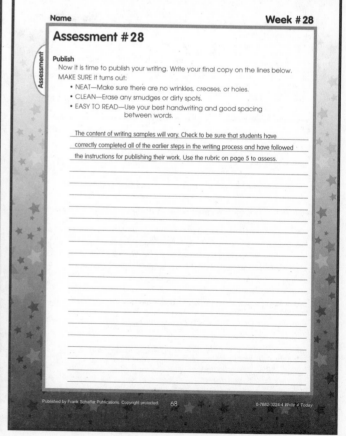

Name — Week # 28

Assessment # 28

Publish

Now it is time to publish your writing. Write your final copy on the lines below. MAKE SURE it turns out:
- NEAT—Make sure there are no wrinkles, creases, or holes.
- CLEAN—Erase any smudges or dirty spots.
- EASY TO READ—Use your best handwriting and good spacing between words.

<u>The content of writing samples will vary. Check to be sure that students have correctly completed all of the earlier steps in the writing process and have followed the instructions for publishing their work. Use the rubric on page 5 to assess.</u>

Answer Key

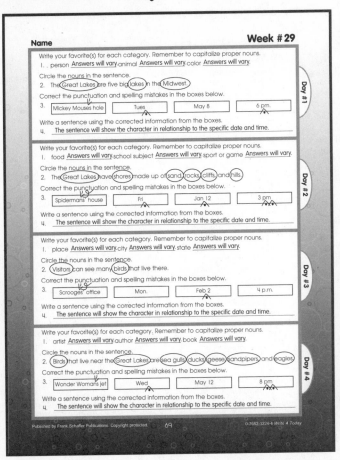

Week # 29

Day #1

Write your favorite(s) for each category. Remember to capitalize proper nouns.
1. person _Answers will vary._ animal _Answers will vary._ color _Answers will vary._

Circle the nouns in the sentence.
2. The (Great Lakes) are five big (lakes) in the (Midwest).

Correct the punctuation and spelling mistakes in the boxes below.
3. | Mickey Mouses hole | Tues | May 8 | 6 p.m. |

Write a sentence using the corrected information from the boxes.
4. _The sentence will show the character in relationship to the specific date and time._

Day #2

Write your favorite(s) for each category. Remember to capitalize proper nouns.
1. food _Answers will vary._ school subject _Answers will vary._ sport or game _Answers will vary._

Circle the nouns in the sentence.
2. The (Great Lakes) have (shores) made up of (sand), (rocks), (cliffs), and (hills).

Correct the punctuation and spelling mistakes in the boxes below.
3. | Spidermans house | Fri | Jan 12 | 3 pm |

Write a sentence using the corrected information from the boxes.
4. _The sentence will show the character in relationship to the specific date and time._

Day #3

Write your favorite(s) for each category. Remember to capitalize proper nouns.
1. place _Answers will vary._ city _Answers will vary._ state _Answers will vary._

Circle the nouns in the sentence.
2. (Visitors) can see many (birds) that live there.

Correct the punctuation and spelling mistakes in the boxes below.
3. | Scrooges office | Mon. | Feb 2 | 4 p.m. |

Write a sentence using the corrected information from the boxes.
4. _The sentence will show the character in relationship to the specific date and time._

Day #4

Write your favorite(s) for each category. Remember to capitalize proper nouns.
1. artist _Answers will vary._ author _Answers will vary._ book _Answers will vary._

Circle the nouns in the sentence.
2. (Birds) that live near the (Great Lakes) are (sea gulls), (ducks), (geese), (sandpipers), and (eagles).

Correct the punctuation and spelling mistakes in the boxes below.
3. | Wonder Womans jet | Wed | May 12 | 8 pm |

Write a sentence using the corrected information from the boxes.
4. _The sentence will show the character in relationship to the specific date and time._

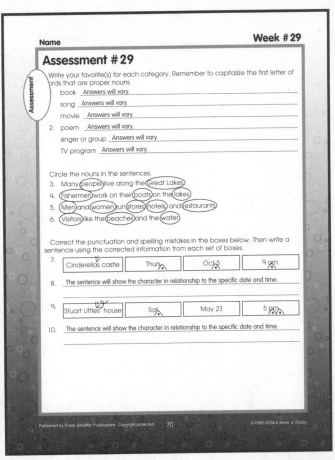

Week # 29

Assessment # 29

Write your favorite(s) for each category. Remember to capitalize the first letter of words that are proper nouns.
1. book _Answers will vary._
   song _Answers will vary._
   movie _Answers will vary._
2. poem _Answers will vary._
   singer or group _Answers will vary._
   TV program _Answers will vary._

Circle the nouns in the sentences.
3. Many (people) live along the (Great Lakes).
4. (Fishermen) work on their (boats) on the (lakes).
5. (Men) and (women) run (stores), (hotels), and (restaurants).
6. (Visitors) like the (beaches) and the (water).

Correct the punctuation and spelling mistakes in the boxes below. Then write a sentence using the corrected information from each set of boxes.

7. | Cinderellas castle | Thurs | Oct 5 | 9 a.m. |

8. _The sentence will show the character in relationship to the specific date and time._

9. | Stuart Littles house | Sat | May 23 | 5 pm |

10. _The sentence will show the character in relationship to the specific date and time._

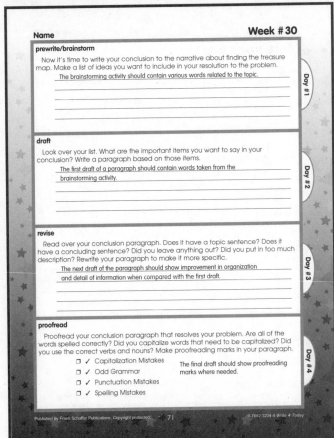

Week # 30

prewrite/brainstorm

Now it's time to write your conclusion to the narrative about finding the treasure map. Make a list of ideas you want to include in your resolution to the problem.
The brainstorming activity should contain various words related to the topic.

Day #1

draft

Look over your list. What are the important items you want to say in your conclusion? Write a paragraph based on those items.
The first draft of a paragraph should contain words taken from the brainstorming activity.

Day #2

revise

Read over your conclusion paragraph. Does it have a topic sentence? Does it have a concluding sentence? Did you leave anything out? Did you put in too much description? Rewrite your paragraph to make it more specific.
The next draft of the paragraph should show improvement in organization and detail of information when compared with the first draft.

Day #3

proofread

Proofread your conclusion paragraph that resolves your problem. Are all of the words spelled correctly? Did you capitalize words that need to be capitalized? Did you use the correct verbs and nouns? Make proofreading marks in your paragraph.
- ☐ ✓ Capitalization Mistakes
- ☐ ✓ Odd Grammar
- ☐ ✓ Punctuation Mistakes
- ☐ ✓ Spelling Mistakes

The final draft should show proofreading marks where needed.

Day #4

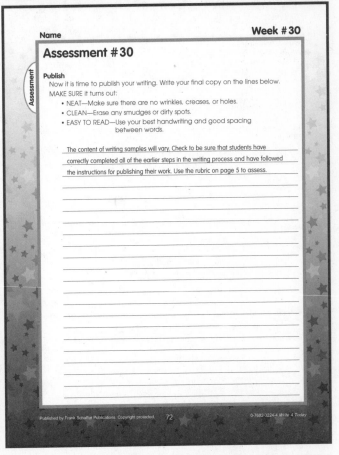

Week # 30

Assessment # 30

Publish

Now it is time to publish your writing. Write your final copy on the lines below. MAKE SURE it turns out:
- NEAT—Make sure there are no wrinkles, creases, or holes.
- CLEAN—Erase any smudges or dirty spots.
- EASY TO READ—Use your best handwriting and good spacing between words.

The content of writing samples will vary. Check to be sure that students have correctly completed all of the earlier steps in the writing process and have followed the instructions for publishing their work. Use the rubric on page 5 to assess.

Answer Key

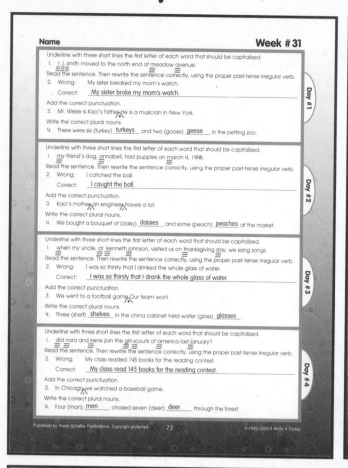

Name   Week # 31

Day #1

Underline with three short lines the first letter of each word that should be capitalized.
1. r. j. smith moved to the north end of meadow avenue.

Read the sentence. Then rewrite the sentence correctly, using the proper past-tense irregular verb.
2. Wrong: My sister breaked my mom's watch.
   Correct: My sister broke my mom's watch.

Add the correct punctuation.
3. Mr. Weise is Kaci's father. He is a musician in New York.

Write the correct plural nouns.
4. There were six (turkey) turkeys and two (goose) geese in the petting zoo.

Day #2

Underline with three short lines the first letter of each word that should be capitalized.
1. my friend's dog, annabell, had puppies on march 4, 1998.

Read the sentence. Then rewrite the sentence correctly, using the proper past-tense irregular verb.
2. Wrong: I catched the ball.
   Correct: I caught the ball.

Add the correct punctuation.
3. Kaci's mother, an engineer, travels a lot.

Write the correct plural nouns.
4. We bought a bouquet of (daisy) daisies and some (peach) peaches at the market.

Day #3

Underline with three short lines the first letter of each word that should be capitalized.
1. when my uncle, dr. kenneth johnson, visited us on thanksgiving day, we sang songs.

Read the sentence. Then rewrite the sentence correctly, using the proper past-tense irregular verb.
2. Wrong: I was so thirsty that I drinked the whole glass of water.
   Correct: I was so thirsty that I drank the whole glass of water.

Add the correct punctuation.
3. We went to a football game. Our team won!

Write the correct plural nouns.
4. Three (shelf) shelves in the china cabinet held water (glass) glasses .

Day #4

Underline with three short lines the first letter of each word that should be capitalized.
1. did nora and irene join the girl scouts of america last january?

Read the sentence. Then rewrite the sentence correctly, using the proper past-tense irregular verb.
2. Wrong: My class readed 145 books for the reading contest.
   Correct: My class read 145 books for the reading contest.

Add the correct punctuation.
3. In Chicago, we watched a baseball game.

Write the correct plural nouns.
4. Four (man) men chased seven (deer) deer through the forest.

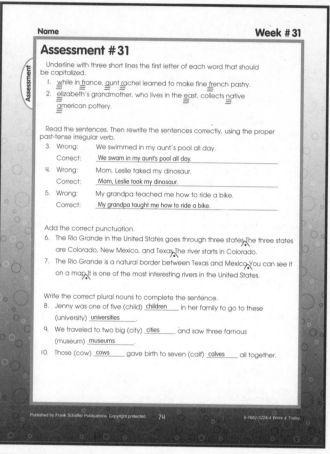

Name   Week # 31

Assessment #31

Underline with three short lines the first letter of each word that should be capitalized.
1. while in france, aunt rachel learned to make fine french pastry.
2. elizabeth's grandmother, who lives in the east, collects native american pottery.

Read the sentences. Then rewrite the sentences correctly, using the proper past-tense irregular verb.
3. Wrong: We swimmed in my aunt's pool all day.
   Correct: We swam in my aunt's pool all day.
4. Wrong: Mom, Leslie taked my dinosaur.
   Correct: Mom, Leslie took my dinosaur.
5. Wrong: My grandpa teached me how to ride a bike.
   Correct: My grandpa taught me how to ride a bike.

Add the correct punctuation.
6. The Rio Grande in the United States goes through three states. The three states are Colorado, New Mexico, and Texas. The river starts in Colorado.
7. The Rio Grande is a natural border between Texas and Mexico. You can see it on a map. It is one of the most interesting rivers in the United States.

Write the correct plural nouns to complete the sentence.
8. Jenny was one of five (child) children in her family to go to these (university) universities .
9. We traveled to two big (city) cities and saw three famous (museum) museums .
10. Those (cow) cows gave birth to seven (calf) calves all together.

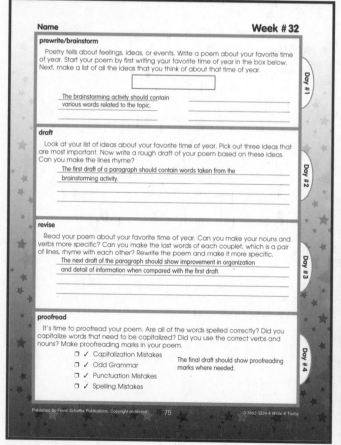

Name   Week # 32

Day #1

prewrite/brainstorm

Poetry tells about feelings, ideas, or events. Write a poem about your favorite time of year. Start your poem by first writing your favorite time of year in the box below. Next, make a list of all the ideas that you think of about that time of year.

The brainstorming activity should contain various words related to the topic.

Day #2

draft

Look at your list of ideas about your favorite time of year. Pick out three ideas that are most important. Now write a rough draft of your poem based on these ideas. Can you make the lines rhyme?

The first draft of a paragraph should contain words taken from the brainstorming activity.

Day #3

revise

Read your poem about your favorite time of year. Can you make your nouns and verbs more specific? Can you make the last words of each couplet, which is a pair of lines, rhyme with each other? Rewrite the poem and make it more specific.

The next draft of the paragraph should show improvement in organization and detail of information when compared with the first draft.

Day #4

proofread

It's time to proofread your poem. Are all of the words spelled correctly? Did you capitalize words that need to be capitalized? Did you use the correct verbs and nouns? Make proofreading marks in your poem.

☐ ✓ Capitalization Mistakes
☐ ✓ Odd Grammar
☐ ✓ Punctuation Mistakes
☐ ✓ Spelling Mistakes

The final draft should show proofreading marks where needed.

Name   Week # 32

Assessment #32

Publish

Now it is time to publish your writing. Write your final copy on the lines below. MAKE SURE it turns out:
- NEAT—Make sure there are no wrinkles, creases, or holes.
- CLEAN—Erase any smudges or dirty spots.
- EASY TO READ—Use your best handwriting and good spacing between words.

The content of writing samples will vary. Check to be sure that students have correctly completed all of the earlier steps in the writing process and have followed the instructions for publishing their work. Use the rubric on page 5 to assess.

Answer Key

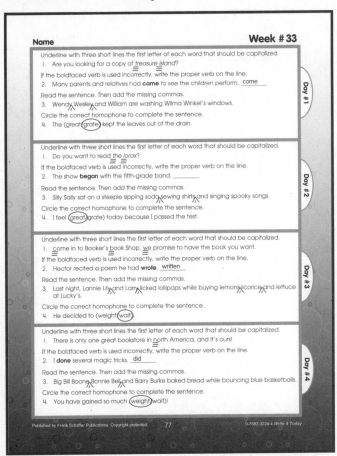

Day #1

Underline with three short lines the first letter of each word that should be capitalized.
1. Are you looking for a copy of *treasure island*?

If the boldfaced verb is used incorrectly, write the proper verb on the line.
2. Many parents and relatives had **came** to see the children perform. __come__

Read the sentence. Then add the missing commas.
3. Wendy, Wesley, and William are washing Wilma Winkel's windows.

Circle the correct homophone to complete the sentence.
4. The (great (grate)) kept the leaves out of the drain.

Day #2

Underline with three short lines the first letter of each word that should be capitalized.
1. Do you want to read *the lorax*?

If the boldfaced verb is used incorrectly, write the proper verb on the line.
2. The show **began** with the fifth-grade band. _____

Read the sentence. Then add the missing commas.
3. Silly Sally sat on a steeple sipping soda, sewing shirts, and singing spooky songs.

Circle the correct homophone to complete the sentence.
4. I feel ((great) grate) today because I passed the test.

Day #3

Underline with three short lines the first letter of each word that should be capitalized.
1. Come in to Booker's book Shop. We promise to have the book you want.

If the boldfaced verb is used incorrectly, write the proper verb on the line.
2. Hector recited a poem he had **wrote**. __written__

Read the sentence. Then add the missing commas.
3. Last night, Lannie, Lily, and Larry licked lollipops while buying lemons, licorice, and lettuce at Lucky's.

Circle the correct homophone to complete the sentence.
4. He decided to (weight (wait)).

Day #4

Underline with three short lines the first letter of each word that should be capitalized.
1. There is only one great bookstore in north America, and it's ours!

If the boldfaced verb is used incorrectly, write the proper verb on the line.
2. I **done** several magic tricks. __did__

Read the sentence. Then add the missing commas.
3. Big Bill Boone, Bonnie Bell, and Barry Burke baked bread while bouncing blue basketballs.

Circle the correct homophone to complete the sentence.
4. You have gained so much ((weight) wait)!

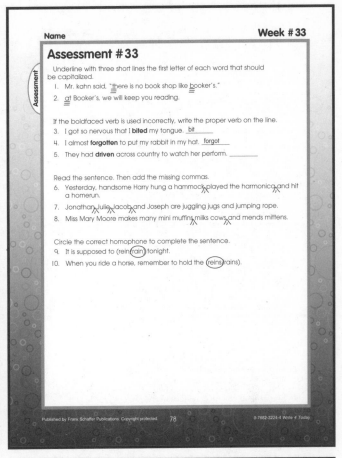

Assessment # 33

Assessment

Underline with three short lines the first letter of each word that should be capitalized.
1. Mr. kahn said, "there is no book shop like booker's."
2. At Booker's, we will keep you reading.

If the boldfaced verb is used incorrectly, write the proper verb on the line.
3. I got so nervous that I **bited** my tongue. __bit__
4. I almost **forgotten** to put my rabbit in my hat. __forgot__
5. They had **driven** across country to watch her perform. _____

Read the sentence. Then add the missing commas.
6. Yesterday, handsome Harry hung a hammock, played the harmonica, and hit a homerun.
7. Jonathan, Julie, Jacob, and Joseph are juggling jugs and jumping rope.
8. Miss Mary Moore makes many mini muffins, milks cows, and mends mittens.

Circle the correct homophone to complete the sentence.
9. It is supposed to (rein (rain)) tonight.
10. When you ride a horse, remember to hold the ((reins) rains).

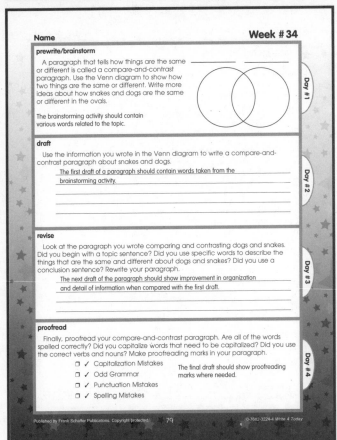

Day #1

prewrite/brainstorm

A paragraph that tells how things are the same or different is called a compare-and-contrast paragraph. Use the Venn diagram to show how two things are the same or different. Write more ideas about how snakes and dogs are the same or different in the ovals.

The brainstorming activity should contain various words related to the topic.

Day #2

draft

Use the information you wrote in the Venn diagram to write a compare-and-contrast paragraph about snakes and dogs.

The first draft of a paragraph should contain words taken from the brainstorming activity.

Day #3

revise

Look at the paragraph you wrote comparing and contrasting dogs and snakes. Did you begin with a topic sentence? Did you use specific words to describe the things that are the same and different about dogs and snakes? Did you use a conclusion sentence? Rewrite your paragraph.

The next draft of the paragraph should show improvement in organization and detail of information when compared with the first draft.

Day #4

proofread

Finally, proofread your compare-and-contrast paragraph. Are all of the words spelled correctly? Did you capitalize words that need to be capitalized? Did you use the correct verbs and nouns? Make proofreading marks in your paragraph.

☐ ✓ Capitalization Mistakes
☐ ✓ Odd Grammar
☐ ✓ Punctuation Mistakes
☐ ✓ Spelling Mistakes

The final draft should show proofreading marks where needed.

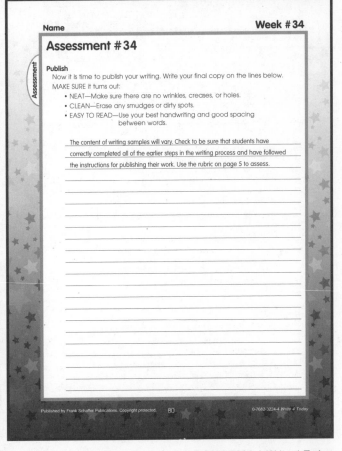

Assessment # 34

Assessment

Publish

Now it is time to publish your writing. Write your final copy on the lines below. MAKE SURE it turns out:
- NEAT—Make sure there are no wrinkles, creases, or holes.
- CLEAN—Erase any smudges or dirty spots.
- EASY TO READ—Use your best handwriting and good spacing between words.

The content of writing samples will vary. Check to be sure that students have correctly completed all of the earlier steps in the writing process and have followed the instructions for publishing their work. Use the rubric on page 5 to assess.

Answer Key

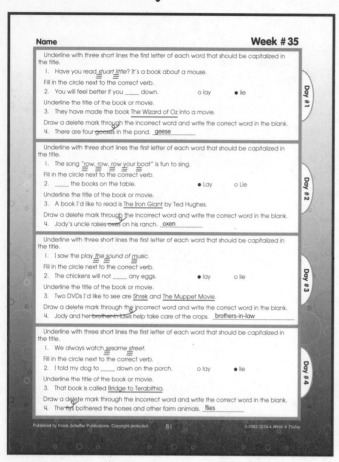

Name   **Week # 35**

Day #1

Underline with three short lines the first letter of each word that should be capitalized in the title.
1. Have you read *stuart little*? It's a book about a mouse.

Fill in the circle next to the correct verb.
2. You will feel better if you _____ down.   o lay   ● lie

Underline the title of the book or movie.
3. They have made the book The Wizard of Oz into a movie.

Draw a delete mark through the incorrect word and write the correct word in the blank.
4. There are four ~~gooses~~ in the pond. _geese_

Day #2

Underline with three short lines the first letter of each word that should be capitalized in the title.
1. The song "row, row, row your boat" is fun to sing.

Fill in the circle next to the correct verb.
2. _____ the books on the table.   ● Lay   o Lie

Underline the title of the book or movie.
3. A book I'd like to read is The Iron Giant by Ted Hughes.

Draw a delete mark through the incorrect word and write the correct word in the blank.
4. Jody's uncle raises ~~oxes~~ on his ranch. _oxen_

Day #3

Underline with three short lines the first letter of each word that should be capitalized in the title.
1. I saw the play *the sound of music.*

Fill in the circle next to the correct verb.
2. The chickens will not _____ any eggs.   ● lay   o lie

Underline the title of the book or movie.
3. Two DVDs I'd like to see are Shrek and The Muppet Movie.

Draw a delete mark through the incorrect word and write the correct word in the blank.
4. Jody and her ~~brother-in-laws~~ help take care of the crops. _brothers-in-law_

Day #4

Underline with three short lines the first letter of each word that should be capitalized in the title.
1. We always watch *sesame street.*

Fill in the circle next to the correct verb.
2. I told my dog to _____ down on the porch.   o lay   ● lie

Underline the title of the book or movie.
3. That book is called Bridge to Terabithia.

Draw a delete mark through the incorrect word and write the correct word in the blank.
4. The ~~flys~~ bothered the horses and other farm animals. _flies_

Published by Frank Schaffer Publications. Copyright protected.   81   0-7682-3224-4 *Write 4 Today*

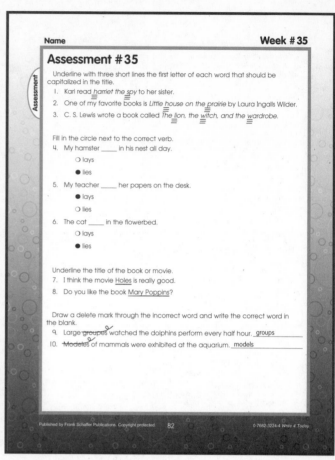

Name   **Week # 35**

Assessment

Assessment # 35

Underline with three short lines the first letter of each word that should be capitalized in the title.
1. Karl read *harriet the spy* to her sister.
2. One of my favorite books is *Little house on the prairie* by Laura Ingalls Wilder.
3. C. S. Lewis wrote a book called *The lion, the witch, and the wardrobe.*

Fill in the circle next to the correct verb.
4. My hamster _____ in his nest all day.
   O lays
   ● lies

5. My teacher _____ her papers on the desk.
   ● lays
   O lies

6. The cat _____ in the flowerbed.
   O lays
   ● lies

Underline the title of the book or movie.
7. I think the movie Holes is really good.
8. Do you like the book Mary Poppins?

Draw a delete mark through the incorrect word and write the correct word in the blank.
9. Large ~~groupes~~ watched the dolphins perform every half hour. _groups_
10. ~~Modeles~~ of mammals were exhibited at the aquarium. _models_

Published by Frank Schaffer Publications. Copyright protected.   82   0-7682-3224-4 *Write 4 Today*

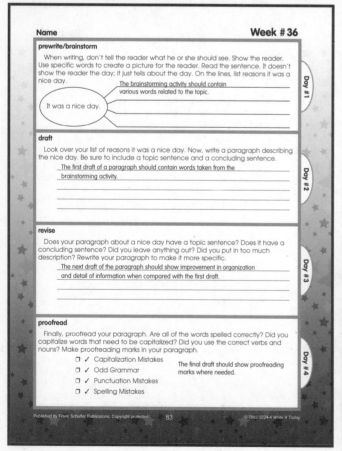

Name   **Week # 36**

Day #1

prewrite/brainstorm

When writing, don't tell the reader what he or she should see. Show the reader. Use specific words to create a picture for the reader. Read the sentence. It doesn't show the reader the day; it just tells about the day. On the lines, list reasons it was a nice day.

It was a nice day.

The brainstorming activity should contain various words related to the topic.

Day #2

draft

Look over your list of reasons it was a nice day. Now, write a paragraph describing the nice day. Be sure to include a topic sentence and a concluding sentence.

The first draft of a paragraph should contain words taken from the brainstorming activity.

Day #3

revise

Does your paragraph about a nice day have a topic sentence? Does it have a concluding sentence? Did you leave anything out? Did you put in too much description? Rewrite your paragraph to make it more specific.

The next draft of the paragraph should show improvement in organization and detail of information when compared with the first draft.

Day #4

proofread

Finally, proofread your paragraph. Are all of the words spelled correctly? Did you capitalize words that need to be capitalized? Did you use the correct verbs and nouns? Make proofreading marks in your paragraph.
   ☐ ✓ Capitalization Mistakes
   ☐ ✓ Odd Grammar
   ☐ ✓ Punctuation Mistakes
   ☐ ✓ Spelling Mistakes

The final draft should show proofreading marks where needed.

Published by Frank Schaffer Publications. Copyright protected.   83   0-7682-3224-4 *Write 4 Today*

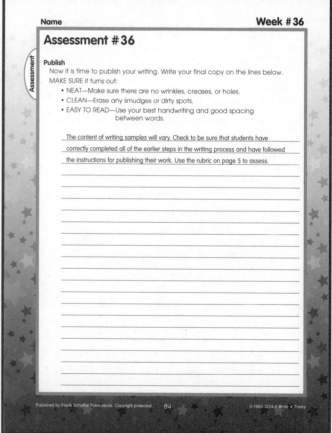

Name   **Week # 36**

Assessment

Assessment # 36

Publish

Now it is time to publish your writing. Write your final copy on the lines below.
MAKE SURE it turns out:
- NEAT—Make sure there are no wrinkles, creases, or holes.
- CLEAN—Erase any smudges or dirty spots.
- EASY TO READ—Use your best handwriting and good spacing between words.

The content of writing samples will vary. Check to be sure that students have correctly completed all of the earlier steps in the writing process and have followed the instructions for publishing their work. Use the rubric on page 5 to assess.

Published by Frank Schaffer Publications. Copyright protected.   84   0-7682-3224-4 *Write 4 Today*

Answer Key

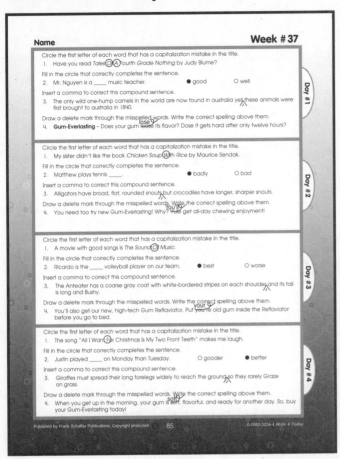

Name — Week # 37

Day #1

Circle the first letter of each word that has a capitalization mistake in the title.
1. Have you read *Tales (O)f (A) Fourth Grade Nothing* by Judy Blume?

Fill in the circle that correctly completes the sentence.
2. Mr. Nguyen is a ____ music teacher. ● good ○ well

Insert a comma to correct this compound sentence.
3. The only wild one-hump camels in the world are now found in australia yet these animals were first brought to australia in 1840.

Draw a delete mark through the misspelled words. Write the correct spelling above them.
4. Gum-Everlasting – Does your gum ~~lose~~ *lose* its flavor? Dose it gets hard after only twelve hours?

Day #2

Circle the first letter of each word that has a capitalization mistake in the title.
1. My sister didn't like the book *Chicken Soup (W)ith Rice* by Maurice Sendak.

Fill in the circle that correctly completes the sentence.
2. Matthew plays tennis ____. ● badly ○ bad

Insert a comma to correct this compound sentence.
3. Alligators have broad, flat, rounded snouts, but crocodiles have longer, sharper snouts.

Draw a delete mark through the misspelled words. Write the correct spelling above them.
4. You need too try new Gum-Everlasting! Why? *you'll* get all-day chewing enjoyment!

Day #3

Circle the first letter of each word that has a capitalization mistake in the title.
1. A movie with good songs is *The Sound (O)f Music.*

Fill in the circle that correctly completes the sentence.
2. Ricardo is the ____ volleyball player on our team. ● best ○ worse

Insert a comma to correct this compound sentence.
3. The Anteater has a coarse gray coat with white-bordered stripes on each shoulder, and its tail is long and Bushy.

Draw a delete mark through the misspelled words. Write the correct spelling above them.
4. You'll also get our new, high-tech Gum Reflaviator. Put *your* old gum inside the Reflaviator before you go to bed.

Day #4

Circle the first letter of each word that has a capitalization mistake in the title.
1. The song "All I Want (F)or Christmas Is My Two Front Teeth" makes me laugh.

Fill in the circle that correctly completes the sentence.
2. Justin played ____ on Monday than Tuesday. ○ gooder ● better

Insert a comma to correct this compound sentence.
3. Giraffes must spread their long forelegs widely to reach the ground, so they rarely Graze on grass.

Draw a delete mark through the misspelled words. Write the correct spelling above them.
4. When you get up in the morning, your gum is *soft*, flavorful, and ready for another day. So, buy your Gum-Everlasting today!

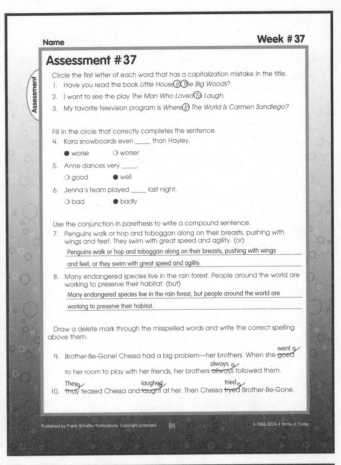

Name — Week # 37

Assessment

Assessment #37

Circle the first letter of each word that has a capitalization mistake in the title.
1. Have you read the book *Little House (I)n (T)he Big Woods?*
2. I want to see the play *The Man Who Loved (T)o Laugh.*
3. My favorite television program is *Where (I)n The World Is Carmen Sandiego?*

Fill in the circle that correctly completes the sentence.
4. Kara snowboards even ____ than Hayley.
   ● worse ○ worser
5. Anne dances very ____.
   ○ good ● well
6. Jenna's team played ____ last night.
   ○ bad ● badly

Use the conjunction in parethesis to write a compound sentence.
7. Penguins walk or hop and toboggan along on their breasts, pushing with wings and feet. They swim with great speed and agility. (or)
   Penguins walk or hop and toboggan along on their breasts, pushing with wings and feet, or they swim with great speed and agility.
8. Many endangered species live in the rain forest. People around the world are working to preserve their habitat. (but)
   Many endangered species live in the rain forest, but people around the world are working to preserve their habitat.

Draw a delete mark through the misspelled words and write the correct spelling above them.
9. Brother-Be-Gone! Chessa had a big problem—her brothers. When she ~~goed~~ *went* to her room to play with her friends, her brothers ~~always~~ *always* followed them.
10. ~~Thay~~ *They* teased Chessa and ~~laught~~ *laughed* at her. Then Chessa ~~tryed~~ *tried* Brother-Be-Gone.

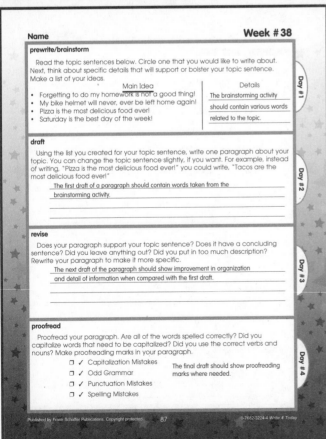

Name — Week # 38

Day #1

prewrite/brainstorm

Read the topic sentences below. Circle one that you would like to write about. Next, think about specific details that will support or bolster your topic sentence. Make a list of your ideas.

Main Idea	Details
• Forgetting to do my homework is not a good thing!	The brainstorming activity
• My bike helmet will never, ever be left home again!	should contain various words
• Pizza is the most delicious food ever!	related to the topic.
• Saturday is the best day of the week!	

Day #2

draft

Using the list you created for your topic sentence, write one paragraph about your topic. You can change the topic sentence slightly, if you want. For example, instead of writing, "Pizza is the most delicious food ever!" you could write, "Tacos are the most delicious food ever!"

The first draft of a paragraph should contain words taken from the brainstorming activity.

Day #3

revise

Does your paragraph support your topic sentence? Does it have a concluding sentence? Did you leave anything out? Did you put in too much description? Rewrite your paragraph to make it more specific.

The next draft of the paragraph should show improvement in organization and detail of information when compared with the first draft.

Day #4

proofread

Proofread your paragraph. Are all of the words spelled correctly? Did you capitalize words that need to be capitalized? Did you use the correct verbs and nouns? Make proofreading marks in your paragraph.

☐ ✓ Capitalization Mistakes
☐ ✓ Odd Grammar
☐ ✓ Punctuation Mistakes
☐ ✓ Spelling Mistakes

The final draft should show proofreading marks where needed.

Name — Week # 38

Assessment

Assessment #38

Publish

Now it is time to publish your writing. Write your final copy on the lines below. MAKE SURE it turns out:
• NEAT—Make sure there are no wrinkles, creases, or holes.
• CLEAN—Erase any smudges or dirty spots.
• EASY TO READ—Use your best handwriting and good spacing between words.

The content of writing samples will vary. Check to be sure that students have correctly completed all of the earlier steps in the writing process and have followed the instructions for publishing their work. Use the rubric on page 5 to assess.

Answer Key

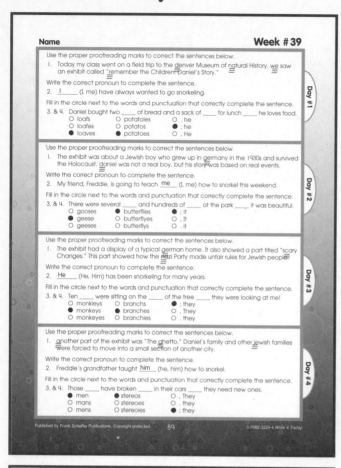

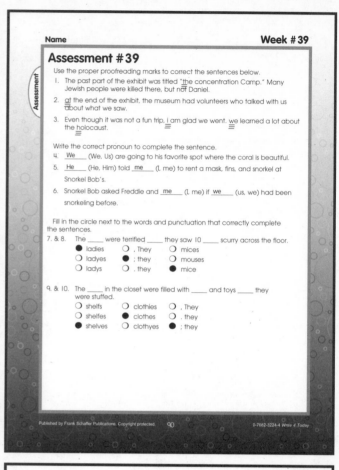

0-7682-3224-4 *Write 4 Today*